AMAZING ANIMALS OF THE WORLD 2

Volume 6

Locust, Migratory — Newt, Crested

GROLIER

First published 2005 by Grolier, an imprint of Scholastic Library Publishing

© 2005 Scholastic Library Publishing

For information address the publisher: Grolier, Scholastic Library Publishing
90 Old Sherman Turnpike
Danbury, CT 06816

Set ISBN: 0-7172-6112-3; Volume ISBN: 0-7172-6118-2

Printed and bound in the U.S.A.

Library of Congress Cataloging-in-Publications Data:
Amazing animals of the world 2.
p.cm.
Includes indexes.
Contents: v. 1. Adder—Buffalo, Water -- v. 2. Bunting, Corn—Cricket, Bush -- v. 3. Cricket, European Mole—Frog, Agile -- v. 4. Frog, Burrowing Tree—Guenon, Moustached -- v. 5. Gull, Great Black-backed—Loach, Stone -- v. 6. Locust, Migratory—Newt, Crested -- v. 7. Nuthatch, Eurasian—Razor, Pod -- v. 8. Reedbuck, Mountain—Snake, Tentacled -- v. 9. Snakefly—Toad, Surinam -- v. 10. Tortoise, Gopher—Zebu.
ISBN 0-7172-6112-3 (set : alk. paper) -- ISBN 0-7172-6113-1 (v. 1 : alk. paper) -- ISBN 0-7172-6114-X (v. 2 : alk. paper) -- ISBN 0-7172-6115-8 (v. 3 : alk. paper) -- ISBN 0-7172-6116-6 (v. 4 : alk. paper) -- ISBN 0-7172-6117-4 (v. 5 : alk. paper) -- ISBN 0-7172-6118-2 (v. 6 : alk. paper) -- ISBN 0-7172-6119-0 (v. 7 : alk. paper) -- ISBN 0-7172-6120-4 (v. 8 : alk. paper) -- ISBN 0-7172-6121-2 (v. 9 : alk. paper) -- ISBN 0-7172-6122-0 (v. 10 : alk.paper)
1. Animals--Juvenile literature. I. Title: Amazing animals of the world two. II. Grolier (Firm)
QL49.A455 2005
590--dc22

2005040351

About This Set

Amazing Animals of the World 2 brings you pictures of 400 fascinating creatures and important information about how and where they live.

Each page shows just one species—individual type—of animal. They all fall into seven main categories or groups of animals (classes and phylums scientifically) that appear on each page as an icon or picture—amphibians, arthropods, birds, fish, mammals, other invertebrates, and reptiles. Short explanations of what these group names mean, and other terms used commonly in the set, appear on page 4 in the Glossary.

Scientists use all kinds of groupings to help them sort out the thousands of types of animals that exist today and once wandered here (extinct species). Kingdoms, classes, phylums, genus, and species are among the key words here that are also explained in the Glossary (page 4).

Where animals live is important to know as well. Each of the species in this set lives in a particular place in the world, which you can see outlined on the map on each page. And in those locales the animals tend to favor a particular habitat—an environment the animal finds suitable for life, with food, shelter, and safety from predators that might eat it. There they also find ways to coexist with other animals in the area that might eat somewhat different food, use different homes, and so on. Each of the main habitats is named on the page and given an icon/picture to help you envision it. The habitat names are further

defined in the Glossary on page 4.

As well as being part of groups like species, animals fall into other categories that help us understand their lives or behavior. You will find these categories in the Glossary on page 4, where you will learn about carnivores, herbivores, and other types of animals.

And there is more information you might want about an animal—its size, diet, where it lives, and how it carries on its species—the way it creates its young. All these facts and more appear in the data boxes at the top of each page.

Finally, you should know that the set is arranged alphabetically by the most common name of the species. That puts most beetles, say, together in a group so you can compare them easily.

But some animals' names are not so common, and they don't appear near others like them. For instance, the chamois is a kind of goat or antelope. To find animals that are similar—or to locate any species—look in the index at the end of each book in the set (pages 45-48). It lists all animals by their various names (you will find the giant South American river turtle under turtle, giant South American river, and also under its other name— arrau). And you will find all birds, fish, and so on gathered under their broader groupings.

Similarly, smaller like groups appear in the set index as well—butterflies include swallowtails and blues, for example.

Table of Contents
Volume 6

Glossary..4

Locust, Migratory..5

Lorikeet, Musk...6

Louse, Human-body..7

Lungfish, Australian..8

Macaque, Crab-eating..9

Macaque, Japanese...10

Macaw, Blue-and-yellow...11

Macaw, Military...12

Magpie, Azure-winged...13

Mamba, Black..14

Manakin, Red-capped..15

Marmot, Olympic...16

Martin, Sand..17

Measurer, Water...18

Merganser, Red-breasted..19

Mink, European..20

Minnow, Eurasian..21

Mole, European..22

Moloch...23

Mongoose, Dwarf..24

Mongoose, White-tailed..25

Monitor, Cape..26

Monitor, Desert..27

Monitor, Gould's..28

Monitor, Nile..29

Monkey, Goeldi's...30

Monkey, Savanna (Grivet)...31

Monkey, Woolly Spider..32

Monster, Gila...33

Mosquito, Eastern Malaria..34

Moth, Common Magpie...35

Moth, Six-spot Burnet...36

Mouflon, European..37

Mouse, Egyptian Spiny..38

Mouse, Wood...39

Mussel, Swan...40

Narwhal...41

Nettle, Sea...42

Newt, Alpine..43

Newt, Crested (Warty Newt)...44

Set Index...45

Glossary

Amphibians—species usually born from eggs in water or wet places, which change (metamorphose) into a land animal. Frogs and salamanders are typical. They breathe through their skin mainly and have no scales.

Arctic and Antarctic—icy, cold, dry areas at the ends of the globe that lack trees but see small plants grown in thawed areas (tundra). Penguins and seals are common inhabitants.

Arthropods—animals with segmented bodies, hard outer skin, and jointed legs, such as spiders and crabs.

Birds—born from eggs, these creatures have wings and often can fly. Eagles, pigeons, and penguins are all birds, though penguins can't fly through the air.

Carnivores—they are animals that eat other animals. Many species do eat each other sometimes, and a few eat dead animals. Lions kill their prey and eat it, while vultures clean up dead bodies of animals.

Cities, Towns, and Farms—places where people live and have built or used the land and share it with many species. Sometimes these animals live in human homes or just nearby.

Class—part or division of a phylum.

Deserts—dry, often warm areas where animals often are more active on cooler nights or near water sources. Owls, scorpions, and jack rabbits are common in American deserts.

Endangered—some animals in this set are marked as endangered because it is possible they will become extinct soon.

Extinct—these species have died out altogether for whatever reason.

Family—part of an order.

Fish—water animals (aquatic) that typically are born from eggs and breathe through gills. Trout and eels are fish, though whales and dolphins are not (they are mammals).

Forests and Mountains—places where evergreen (coniferous) and leaf-shedding (deciduous) trees are common, or that rise in elevation to make cool, separate habitats.

Rainforests are different (see below).

Fresh Water—lakes, rivers, and the like carry fresh water (unlike Oceans and Shores, where the water is salty). Fish and birds abound, as do insects, frogs, and mammals.

Genus—part of a family.

Grasslands—habitats with few trees and light rainfall. Grasslands often lie between forests and deserts, and they are home to birds, coyotes, antelope, and snakes, as well as many other kinds of animals.

Herbivores—these animals eat mainly plants. Typical are hoofed animals (ungulates) that are common on grasslands, such as antelope or deer. Domestic (nonwild) ones are cows and horses.

Hibernators—species that live in harsh areas with very cold winters slow down their functions then and sort of sleep through the hard times.

Kingdom—the largest division of species. Commonly there are understood to be five kingdoms: animals, plants, fungi, protists, and monerans.

Mammals—these creatures usually bear live young and feed them on milk from the mother. A few lay eggs (monotremes like the platypus) or nurse young in a pouch (marsupials like opossums and kangaroos).

Migrators—some species spend different seasons in different places, moving to where more food, warmth, or safety can be found. Birds often do this, sometimes over long distances, but others types of animals also move seasonally, including fish and mammals.

Oceans and Shores—seawater is salty, often deep, and huge. In it live many fish, invertebrates, and even some mammals, such as whales. On the shore birds and other creatures often gather.

Order—part of a class.

Other Invertebrates—animals that lack backbones or internal skeletons. Many, such as insects and shrimp, have hard outer coverings. Clams and worms are also invertebrates.

Phylum—part of a kingdom.

Rainforests—here huge trees grow among many other plants helped by the warm, wet environment. Thousands of species of animals also live in these rich habitats.

Reptiles—these species have scales, lungs to breathe, and lay eggs or give birth to live young. Dinosaurs are thought to have been reptiles, while today the class includes turtles, snakes, lizards, and crocodiles.

Scientific name—the genus and species name of a creature in Latin. For instance, Canis lupus is the wolf. Scientific names avoid the confusion possible with common names in any one language or across languages.

Species—a group of the same type of living thing. Part of an order.

Subspecies—a variant but quite similar part of a species.

Territorial—many animals mark out and defend a patch of ground as their home area. Birds and mammals may call quite small or quite large spots their territories.

Vertebrates—animals with backbones and skeletons under their skins

Migratory Locust
Locusta migratoria

Length: about 2 inches
Wingspan: about 4 inches
Diet: plants
Method of Reproduction: egg
layer

Home: Eurasia and Africa
Order: Grasshoppers and their
relatives
Family: Short-horned
grasshoppers

  Deserts

Arthropods

© KIM TAYLOR / BRUCE COLEMAN INC.

Locusts written about in the Bible were likely either this species, the migratory locust, or its close cousin, the desert locust, *Schistocerca gregaria*. Both are found in Africa and the Middle East, and both form huge swarms that devour all plant life in their path.

Migratory locusts usually live solitary lives widely separated from each other. Every few years, however, they gather together to migrate. Scientists now know that this swarming is triggered by a combination of hot and dry weather conditions and large locust populations.

The locusts' frenzied migration begins when daily temperatures reach 77 degrees Fahrenheit, and their journey continues through the night if temperatures stay high. When they begin to travel, many locusts are still immature, wingless nymphs. These young locusts begin their journey on foot, walking 300 to 350 yards a day. They swim across water and even intertwine their bodies to form a living bridge. Adult migratory locusts gather in great clouds as they fly. Some of these swarms stay close to the ground, while others fly very high.

Swarming locusts are infamous for the enormous amount of plant food they eat each day. A large swarm can consume enough food to feed 1.5 million people! The swarm itself may weigh as much as 15,000 tons.

Musk Lorikeet
Glossopsitta concinna

Length: about 9 inches
Diet: nectar, pollen, blossoms, fruits, seeds, and insects
Number of Eggs: usually 2

Home: southeastern Australia
Order: Parrots
Family: Parrots

 Rainforests

 Birds

© ROLAND SEITRE / PETER ARNOLD, INC.

The musk lorikeet has a bright headband of red feathers that wraps over its bill and around the sides of its head. Despite its colorful markings, a solitary musk lorikeet is difficult to spot in trees. A whole flock of lorikeets, however, is impossible to ignore. Their noisy screeching has been compared to the sound of metal scraping against metal, although, fortunately, the birds quiet down somewhat when they are feeding. But even then they continue to chatter among themselves. Should anything disturb their feast, the screeching immediately resumes.

Like all "lories," musk lorikeets have a brush-tipped tongue designed for lapping up pollen and nectar from tropical flowers.

These lorikeets also have a huge appetite for fruit. This makes farmers angry because the birds often invade orchards and have even been known to devour entire fields of barely ripe corn. These birds are also attracted to farmland because they prefer open areas to thick forests.

Musk lorikeets breed from August to January. Working together, the mated pair cleans out a hollow in a branch or a hole in the trunk of a tree. They line the hole with a layer of soft wood dust, onto which the female lays her eggs. Little else is known about their breeding behavior. Like all lories, this species is very social. Their flocks are large, and they often mingle with other lories and parrots.

Human-body Louse
Pediculus humanus

Length: 1/10 to 1/8 inch
Width: 1/24 inch
Diet: human blood
Number of Eggs: 300

Home: worldwide wherever there are people
Order: Lice
Family: Sucking lice

 Cities, Towns, and Farms

 Arthropods

© EYE OF SCIENCE / PHOTO RESEARCHERS

The human-body louse undoubtedly ranks as one of the least favorite of all animals. It spends its life on a human being's body, gripping the person's hair with its claws and sucking his or her blood.

There are only two kinds of lice that attack humans: the crab louse and the human louse. The human louse is divided into two subspecies. One, the head louse, lives among the hairs of our heads. The other, the body louse, lives on the rest of our bodies and in our clothing and bedding.

Lice are more than just annoying: they also carry deadly diseases such as typhus and relapsing fever. Lice have even influenced the outcomes of wars. Many soldiers in battle zones have become ill after being infested with these disease-carrying insects. Fortunately, human lice have been largely controlled in Western countries. However, there are still occasional outbreaks when people must live together in crowded or unclean conditions.

If you look closely, you can tell the difference between a louse and that other blood-sucking parasite, the flea. Both insects are flat. But the louse is flattened from front to back, like a turtle. The flea is flattened from side to side, like a fish. Unlike fleas, the louse will not move from one kind of animal to another. You may get fleas from your dog, but you won't get lice.

Australian Lungfish
Neoceratodus forsteri

Length: 3 to 5 feet
Weight: 25 to 50 pounds
Method of Reproduction: egg layer

Diet: frogs and small fish
Home: Australia
Order: Lungfishes
Family: Primitive lungfishes

 Fresh Water

 Fish

© REG MORRISON / AUSCAPE / MINDEN PICTURES

As its name implies, the Australian lungfish can breathe air using a primitive set of lungs. But unlike other types of lungfish, this species usually breathes through its gills. Gills extract oxygen that is dissolved in the water. The Australian lungfish uses its lungs only when it finds itself in polluted or silty water. To avoid clogging its gills with dirt or toxins, it swims to the surface, sticks out its head, and gulps in air. The air passes down a simple tube into the fish's lungs.

The Australian lungfish eats in an unusual way as well. It is a predator that has no teeth. After nabbing a juicy frog or minnow, the lungfish slices its meal into strips using two bony plates inside its mouth. The sharp plates work much like scissors.

In summer, the Australian lungfish swims to shallow waters to mate. When a couple meets, the male nudges the female until she scatters her eggs over a thick patch of weeds. He then releases his sperm, which floats over the eggs and fertilizes them.

The Australian lungfish is a primitive animal. That is, the species has changed little in the millions of years it has been on Earth. The Australian lungfish has a pair of fins beneath its body that are like those of prehistoric fish. About 400 million years ago, bottom-dwelling fish used such fins to walk across the mud and sand. These ancient lungfish may have even used their "fin-feet" to occasionally waddle onto land.

Crab-eating Macaque
Macaca fascicularis

Length: 16 to 22 inches
Length of the Tail: 16 to 26 inches
Weight: 11 to 20 pounds (male); 7 to 13 pounds (female)

Diet: insects, plants, and small animals
Number of Young: 1
Home: Southeast Asia
Order: Primates
Family: Old World monkeys

 Rainforests

 Mammals

© PETER HULME / ECOSCENE / CORBIS

Get up early. Spend the morning looking for food. Take a midday nap. Spend several more hours looking for food. Play a little in the late afternoon. Then, as darkness falls, settle down in a favorite sleeping tree for a long night's rest. That's the daily schedule for crab-eating macaques. These monkeys spend most of their time in trees. They have special pads on the buttocks that help cushion their behind during their long periods of sitting. But the macaques also like water. They are often found on seacoasts and rivers, where they can be seen swimming and diving. These primates eat fruit and other plant matter, crabs, mollusks, and other small animals.

Crab-eating macaques live in groups of 20 to 60 individuals. A female spends her entire life in the group into which she was born. By contrast, a male generally moves from group to group. Living in a group has an important advantage: it helps protect the macaques against enemies, since predators will think twice before intruding on a large number of macaques.

The main enemies of crab-eating macaques are tree-climbing predators such as panthers, clouded leopards, and pythons. Crab-eating macaques are more adaptable to the presence of human beings than are most monkeys. The people of Bali believe that the macaques are sacred animals and even bring gifts of food to them.

Japanese Macaque
Macaca fuscata

Length: 2½ to 3 feet
Length of Tail: 4 inches
Diet: fruits, berries, nuts, and insects

Number of Young: 1
Home: Japan
Order: Primates
Family: Old World monkeys

 Forests and Mountains

 Mammals

© WOLFGANG KAEHLER / CORBIS

The Japanese macaque is a large, strong monkey with dark-brown fur and a reddish, hairless face. In the northern part of Japan, where winters are cold and snow is deep, the macaques grow thick fur. They also keep warm by sitting close together and hugging one another. These monkeys eat a varied diet, including plant matter, mushrooms, seaweed, insects and their eggs, spiders, snails, crabs, and bird eggs. In some places, they have developed interesting habits. For instance, some of the macaques on the island of Koshima wash sweet potatoes before eating them, to remove the sand.

The main enemies of Japanese macaques are people. Until about 1950, Japanese macaques were hunted for food and for their fur. Today the animals are protected by law, but their population is still diminishing because people are cutting down the forests in which the animals live.

Japanese macaques are social animals that typically live in groups of 20 to 100 individuals. They spend time both on the ground and in trees, and they are excellent swimmers. When a group travels, the adult males act as leaders and guardians. The females give birth to one offspring in spring or early summer. These primates play a large part in Japanese mythology and folklore, often appearing on old silk screens and ancient manuscripts.

Blue-and-Yellow Macaw
Ara ararauna

Length of the Body: about 34 inches
Length of the Tail: about 20 inches
Diet: fruits, seeds, nuts, and other plant matter

Weight: about 2½ pounds
Number of Eggs: 1 or 2
Home: tropical South America
Order: Parrots
Family: Parrots

Rainforests

Birds

© CORBIS

Many naturalists have marveled at the spectacular flight of the blue-and-yellow macaw. From the ground, the bird's brilliant yellow underfeathers flash in the sun. Even more dramatic is the 20-inch-long tail that streams gracefully behind in flight. From above, the blue upperfeathers provide a sharp contrast to the lush tropical greenery of the South American rainforests.

Fortunately, blue-and-yellow macaws are still quite common in remote parts of the rainforest. However, they quickly disappear from regions where humans cut or burn the forest. These colorful parrots feed in tall trees along rivers and streams. During the dry season, they seldom leave the jungle. But in the rainy season, they fly long distances to feed in grasslands and palm groves.

Outside of breeding season, blue-and-yellow macaws live in large flocks. Each morning the flock rises into the air with tremendous screeching. "Rraaa—aaa" is their cry. The macaws eventually break from the flock and travel to separate feeding areas. Just before sunset, they return to their roosting spot.

Blue-and-yellow macaws mate for life. Although many couples live within a larger flock, each bird stays beside its mate. Between February and June, the mated pairs leave the flock to nest. The female incubates the eggs, while the male guards her and the eggs.

Military Macaw
Ara militaris

Length of the Body: about 28 inches
Weight: about 2½ pounds
Diet: seeds, nuts, berries, fruits, and other plant matter

Number of Eggs: 2
Home: Central and South America
Order: Parrots
Family: Parrots

Forests and Mountains

Birds

The green-and-blue plumage of this colorful macaw reminded European naturalists of the full-dress uniforms worn by military officers. And so the bird was named. Like many other beautiful parrots, military macaws are often killed for their splendid feathers. Poachers also steal the macaw's nestlings to sell as expensive pets. As a result, the military macaw is now rarely found outside of certain remote areas.

Military macaws are usually seen in pairs or in small flocks of up to 20 birds, most often in the dry canyons and thorn forests of Mexico. This species's close cousin, the scarlet macaw, populates Mexico's rainforests and may keep the military macaw from settling there. Military macaws also inhabit tropical regions in Colombia and Venezuela, and they live on the eastern slopes of the Andes Mountains in northern Peru. In September and October, these mountain macaws fly over high peaks and grasslands to visit fruit-filled forests near the Pacific coast.

Wherever they live, military macaws greet each morning with raucous screeching. "Kraa—aak!" they shout. In the early light, flocks rise up from their roosting sites and fly to their feeding areas. Within each flock the mated pairs remain close to each other. Like many parrots, military macaws mate for life. They nest in high tree holes and sometimes adopt empty woodpecker nests.

Azure-winged Magpie
Cyanopica cyana

Length: about 13 inches
Weight: about 2½ ounces
Diet: grain, insects, snails, slugs, and spiders
Number of Eggs: 3 to 7

Home: Spain, Portugal, and eastern Central Asia
Order: Perching birds
Family: Crows, jays, and magpies

 Forests and Mountains

 Birds

© ROGER TIDMAN / CORBIS

The bold and perky azure-winged magpie lives in the gardens, fruit orchards, and olive groves of Spain and Portugal. Large flocks often roam the countryside, filling the air with their noisy chatter. The European variety is widely separated from a much larger population found in eastern Russia, China, and Japan. These Asian azure-winged magpies live in thick forests of oak and conifer trees.

No one knows with certainty how the magpie's two populations came to be so widely separated. In any case, distance now prevents them from intermixing. So they have developed into two races, or subspecies, with slightly different behaviors and appearances. Still, both have a striking black hood and light blue wings and tail. Males and females look similar. And, like many magpies, both have a very long and elegant tail.

After mating in May, azure-winged magpies build an open nest, usually in the fork of a pine, poplar, or oak tree. The female lays up to seven darkly speckled grayish-blue eggs. Great spotted cuckoos often lay an egg in the nest while the magpies are away. The cuckoo chick then relies on its adopted magpie parents for food and care. The cuckoo chick does not kill or starve its foster brothers and sisters. The adult magpies are able to bring enough food for their own chicks and the cuckoo.

Black Mamba
Dendroaspis polylepis

Diet: mainly birds and small
    mammals
Number of Eggs: about 12
Home: eastern and southern
    Africa

Length: 7 to 14 feet
Order: Lizards and snakes
Family: Cobras and their
    relatives

 Grasslands

 Reptiles

© JOE MCDONALD / CORBIS

The black mamba is the largest poisonous snake in Africa and the fastest snake in the world. Once, a black mamba was timed as it chased a man who had been foolhardy enough to tease it. The snake raced along at 7 miles per hour—about twice as fast as any North American snake and double the speed of a brisk human walk!

The black mamba prefers to mind its own business; if disturbed, it tries to escape by crawling into its hole. But if angered or frightened, it is ready to fight and makes a terrifying enemy. The mamba spreads its neck, opens its mouth wide, and hisses. Raising its head high in the air, it glides forward and strikes. Once angered, the mamba is fearless. It will strike at much bigger animals than itself—including humans. Humans would do well to respect the mamba; its venom is highly poisonous, and a single bite will soon kill a person unless antivenin is given quickly. (Antivenin is a medicine that counteracts the venom.) The main purpose of the black mamba's venom is to kill its prey. When looking for food, this snake sometimes climbs trees, but unlike other mambas, it usually stays on the ground. The black mamba is most active during the day.

After mating, the female lays her eggs in a tree hollow or termite nest. The baby mamba uses a tiny egg tooth at the tip of its snout to break through the shell. The egg tooth falls off soon after the baby hatches.

Red-capped Manakin
Pipra mentalis

Length: about 4½ inches
Weight: about ½ ounce
Diet: fruits and insects
Number of Eggs: usually 2

Home: Central and South America
Order: Perching birds
Family: Manakins

 Rainforests

 Birds

© GEORGE D. DODGE & DALE R. THOMPSON / BRUCE COLEMAN INC.

The small, stocky red-capped manakin is at home in the densest parts of the tropical rainforest. As adults, males and females look surprisingly different. The male's bright red head feathers stand out next to the pitch-black feathers on his wings, back, and breast. At the top of his legs, the male wears pure-white "bloomers" made of soft, downy feathers. The female is a very drab olive-green that enables her to disappear in thick jungle vegetation.

The bright colors of the male play an important role in his showy courtship dance. To make a stage for himself, the breeding male strips a branch of all its leaves. He continues smoothing down the branch by nervously pecking and scratching at the bark. Sometimes a second male joins the first. Together, they sing a loud duet, hoping to attract one or more females. When a female does appear, the males jump and twitter with great excitement.

Despite his elaborate show, the male has no lasting loyalty for any one mate. Instead, he tries to breed with as many females as possible. Each of his mates builds her own nest and raises her chicks. Using fine plant fibers, she weaves a delicate basket. Typically she builds the nest in a low bush near a stream or some swampy soil. Although her own diet consists mainly of fruits, the female feeds her chicks a high-protein mash of bugs. This energy-rich diet enables her young to grow quickly.

15

Olympic Marmot
Marmota olympus

Length of the Body: 19 to 21 inches
Length of the Tail: 8 to 10 inches
Diet: mainly grasses, herbs, and roots

Weight : 6 to 24 pounds
Number of Young: 2 to 6
Home: northwestern United States
Order: Rodents
Family: Squirrels

 Forests and Mountains

 Mammals

© LEE RENTZ / BRUCE COLEMAN INC.

Olympic marmots are named for their home, the small Olympic Peninsula of northwestern Washington State. Like most marmots, these "Olympians" live on rocky mountain slopes and high alpine meadows. Marmots are the world's largest squirrels. Their stocky build enables them to live in cold environments.

Like others of its kind, the Olympic marmot is a hardworking excavator. Over many generations a family of marmots will dig an elaborate system of underground tunnels. At the center of the tunnel system, 3 to 6 feet beneath the surface, is a large den, or lodge, filled with soft nesting materials.

Most Olympic marmot families build two separate lodges, one for summer and one for winter. Deep within the winter lodge, the family hibernates, cuddled together for warmth. It is the winter cold, not predators, that kills most Olympic marmots. The easiest winters for survival are those with lots of snow. A thick blanket of snow insulates the marmot's underground den.

Typically each marmot family includes one adult male, two females, and their young offspring. Each female gives birth every other year, and the whole family helps raise the babies. The family members are friendly and often groom each other and sunbathe together.

Sand Martin

Riparia riparia

Length: 4¾ to 5½ inches
Wingspan: 10 to 11 inches
Number of Eggs: usually 4 or 5, but up to 8
Home: *Summer:* North America, Europe, Asia, and northern Africa

Winter: South America, central Africa, and Southeast Asia
Diet: insects
Order: Perching birds
Family: True swallows

 Fresh Water

 Birds

☐ Summer ■ Winter

© JOHN ROBINSON / PETER ARNOLD, INC.

Sand martins are famous for their boundless energy and their lively flight. Twisting and zigzagging through the air, the little bird snaps up winged insects, including flying termites, leafhoppers, and mosquitoes.

Sand martins even court in the air. During their courtship flight, the couple pass a ceremonial white feather back and forth. It is their token of love, so to speak. Once they mate, the pair join with other sand martins and dig a burrow in a shared nesting site. The site is often built in a steep riverbank of sand or gravel. Occasionally sand martins nest along the side of a road or the bank of a railroad track. By nesting together the martins work as a group to fight off predators such as dogs, cats, and

raccoons. These birds will mob an enemy like a squadron of dive-bombers.

Sand martins start their burrows by pecking a small hole. The male and female take turns kicking sand out of the hole until their tunnel is about 3 feet deep. At the end of the burrow, the birds build a nest out of hair, feathers, soft grasses, and roots. The parents take turns warming their eggs for about 16 days. The young are ready to leave the burrow and fly about three weeks after they hatch. By the fall the young sand martins must be ready to migrate with their parents. North American martins fly to South America, while Eurasian flocks (called bank swallows) travel to Africa and southern Asia.

Water Measurer
Hydrometra sp.

Length: about ⅓ inch
Diet: smaller insects and crustaceans
Method of Reproduction: egg layer

Home: North America, Europe, Asia, and northern Africa
Order: True bugs
Family: Water measurers

 Fresh Water

Arthropods

© G. I. BERNARD / OSF / ANIMALS ANIMALS / EARTH SCENES

The small, slender water measurer walks slowly across the water's surface—as if it were carefully marking off each millimeter of the pond. Its head is long and slender, and its legs are as thin as fine needles.

Water measurers are close cousins to the water striders. Both insects are fairly common and often live in the same habitats. It is easy to tell them apart: water measurers slowly walk across the water on six legs, while water striders race along quickly on four. And while water striders boldly skate into the middle of a pond or stream, water measurers stay close to shore.

Water measurers are most common along the edges of ponds and the quiet backwaters of small streams. They also crawl onto plants along the shore, but always breed in water. The female lays her eggs on floating plants or debris.

Water measurers are active predators that hunt tiny insects and crustaceans in the water and on wet plants. Scientists believe that this bug has excellent eyesight. Its large eyes bulge out on either side of its head. The water measurer can also feel for its prey with its long, sensitive antennae. By touching its antennae to the water's surface, it can detect the most minute waves produced when a tiny insect falls onto the water.

Red-breasted Merganser
Mergus serrator

Length: 19 to 26 inches
Weight: about 2 pounds
Diet: fish and crustaceans
Number of Eggs: 9 or 10
Home: Northern Hemisphere

Order: Ducks and screamers
Family: Swans, geese, and ducks
Subfamily: Mergansers

 Fresh Water

 Birds

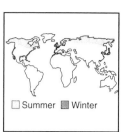
Summer Winter

© HAL BERAL / CORBIS

The male red-breasted merganser is a brightly costumed show-off. During courtship, he literally runs across the surface of the water to catch the attention of a female. Then he performs an elaborate mating ceremony: flapping his wings, dipping his bill, and preening his feathers in a carefully orchestrated display. Despite this great show of affection, the male red-breasted merganser is an irresponsible husband. Once his mate has laid her eggs, the male deserts her. Fortunately, female mergansers have learned to take care of each other. Nesting females gather close together for protection. Then, when their eggs hatch, they gather their chicks into one large brood and tend it together.

Mergansers are all diving, fish-eating ducks. They are meat eaters that have evolved long, sharp bills with serrated edges, much like steak knives. During most of the year, red-breasted mergansers hunt in coastal and inland waters in Canada and northern Russia. In late fall, they migrate down through the United States and Eurasia to winter in warm coastal waters.

The red-breasted merganser resembles the more familiar common merganser, a slightly larger duck. The males of both species have a blackish-green head and a black back, while the females are brown-headed with a gray body. To recognize the red-breasted merganser, look for a spiky head crest.

19

European Mink
Mustela lutreola

Length of the Body: 14 to 17 inches
Length of the Tail: 5¼ to 7½ inches
Weight: 14 to 43 ounces
Diet: small animals

Number of Young: 2 to 7
Home: Europe and western Asia
Order: Carnivores
Family: Mustelids

 Fresh Water

 Mammals

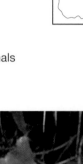

© BIOS / PETER ARNOLD, INC.

Like its American cousin, the European mink has been heavily hunted for centuries. Its value lies in its luxurious fur. American and European minks are very similar, with shiny dark brown to blackish fur. But the European species is somewhat smaller and has shorter fur. The hair around its lips and chin is white. This mink is particularly beautiful in winter, when it grows a thick undercoat.

The mink has disappeared from most of Western Europe due to hunting and loss of habitat. Outside of an isolated area in southern France, it is now found only in Eastern Europe and Russia. European fur farmers seldom raise this species. Instead, they import the long-haired American mink, whose fur is considerably more valuable.

The mink is an agile hunter and is active both day and night. Despite its short legs, it can run quickly and is famous for sneaking up on and attacking its prey. On land the mink's favorite victims are voles, mice, and birds. It also hunts in fresh water—even in the winter, when it dives through holes in the ice. After the mink catches a fish, frog, or crayfish, it carries the prey to shore in its mouth. It may store a large number of animals in its den before eating them.

European mink breed in April. The female gives birth in late May or June. Weighing barely a quarter ounce, the newborn, called pups, nurse for about three months and become independent soon after.

Eurasian Minnow
Phoxinus phoxinus

Length: up to 5½ inches
Diet: mainly insects and insect larvae; also algae
Method of Reproduction: egg layer

Home: Europe and Asia
Order: Carps and their relatives
Family: Carps

 Fresh Water

 Fish

© JANE BURTON / BRUCE COLEMAN INC.

Eurasian minnows are small freshwater fish that live in large groups, or schools. These schools are constantly on the move, prowling the surface of the water in oxygen-rich habitats such as rivers, small streams, ponds, pools, and lakes. If something should disturb the school, its members quickly scatter.

The principal foods of the Eurasian minnow are small invertebrates and algae. Although the fish has teeth, they are not located in its jaws, as one would expect. Instead, the minnow's two rows of teeth are located in its throat! Eurasian minnows are popular prey for larger fish such as trout. Although people sometimes eat these fish, the minnows are more often used as bait.

The Eurasian minnow is a dull grayish silver, but it becomes quite colorful during the breeding season. At that time, its sides turn green, its throat turns black, and its belly becomes a reddish orange. The minnows spawn (lay their eggs) in cool, running water. As the female lays her eggs, the male releases sperm that fertilizes them.

The Eurasian minnow is a popular aquarium fish. It has a lively but peaceful nature and requires very little care. The minnow is even trainable and can be taught to respond to a whistle. If a person whistles each time he or she gives the minnow food, the fish will soon learn to swim to the feeding spot whenever it hears the whistle!

European Mole
Talpa europaea

Length of the Body: 4 to 7 inches

Length of the Tail: about 1 inch

Weight: 2 to 4 ounces

Diet: mainly earthworms

Number of Young: 2 to 9

Home: Europe

Order: Insectivores

Family: Moles

Cities, Towns, and Farms

Mammals

© JEAN-LOUIS LE MOIGNE / PETER ARNOLD, INC.

Like the moles of North America and northern Asia, the common mole of Europe spends most of its life underground. It is especially abundant in the fertile soil of farm pastures, yards, and meadows. The mole's underground world consists of dark, narrow tunnels and nesting chambers.

The European mole's eyes are tiny and nearly useless in its dark environment. However, its senses of hearing, smell, and touch are very keen. The mole can hear an earthworm move from several feet away and can even feel the tiny vibrations made by the worm's movements.

Like North American moles, the European species has broad, shovel-like paws with long, strong claws. Its shoulders and arms are short and massive, designed for powerful digging. During the summer the mole digs its tunnels just beneath the surface. In winter, it burrows deeper to escape the cold. At the center of the mole's network of tunnels is an 8-inch-wide nesting chamber. The animal also builds storage rooms, which it fills with earthworms and other invertebrates. The mole will eat these stored goodies during the winter months, when fresh food is less available.

European moles live alone, except during breeding season. They mate from March to June, and the females give birth to blind, naked babies. The young leave their mother's nest when they are two months old.

Moloch
Moloch horridus

Length: 8 to 9 inches
Diet: ants
Method of Reproduction: egg layer

Home: central Australia
Order: Lizards and snakes
Family: Chisel-teeth lizards

Deserts

Reptiles

The moloch is a lizard that lives only in the Australian desert. The large spiny scales that cover its body and tail give it a dangerous appearance. It looks as if it is wearing armor with spikes. The moloch is, however, a harmless animal that uses its spikes only to protect itself. It lives in the center of the desert and in dry plains. It hides itself by changing its sandy color from red to brown to match the background.

The moloch is a slow-moving lizard that feeds only on black ants. The moloch settles quietly by the side of an ants' trail, licking up the passing insects. It may eat up to 2,000 ants during a meal!

The moloch has a spiny hump of fat at the back of its head where it stores water for dry periods. The camel uses its hump the same way. But the moloch also has another way to use even the smallest drop of water. Its entire body has thin grooves between the scales. These grooves draw water from moist air. The tiny grooves also carry the water to the moloch's mouth so it can drink. The moloch is a very good example of how an animal can change its body to be able to live under harsh conditions. The hump behind the moloch's head also has another use. When a moloch wants to scare an enemy, it bends its head down between its forelegs. Then the hump looks like a second head, which confuses the enemy.

Dwarf Mongoose
Helogale parvula

Length of the Body: 7 to 9 inches
Length of the Tail: up to 7 inches
Diet: mainly insects, also small mammals and reptiles

Weight: up to 12 ounces
Number of Young: 2 to 4
Home: Africa
Order: Carnivores
Family: Viverrids, aardwolves, and hyenas

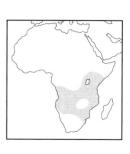

 Grasslands

 Mammals

© JOE MCDONALD / CORBIS

As its name suggests, the dwarf mongoose is Africa's smallest. It is also the best known, because it is not at all shy and runs about during the day, chattering to its relatives. Biologists say that dwarf mongooses have a rich "language" that takes the form of chirping signals. Members of a dwarf mongoose family, which may number up to 50, constantly call to each other, as if to say, "Here I am! Where are you?" Their chattering can be heard up to 200 feet away, even in thick grass.

As it hunts, the mongoose family is always guarded by two sentries. Members take turns standing guard, switching off about every 15 minutes. Should danger approach, the guards cry out, and the entire group vanishes under cover. These very social creatures also cooperate with other animal species. For example, each dwarf mongoose family has an escort of birds, often bright-yellow-billed toucans. The toucans eat some of the grasshoppers that the mongooses stir up from the grass. In return the toucans squawk out a warning should predators such as hawks, falcons, or eagles come near.

The tight-knit dwarf mongoose family is usually governed by a "queen" and her husband. The queen is the only female to have babies, and the whole colony helps raise the young. For its home the family usually adopts an old termite nest or the deserted burrow of another animal.

White-tailed Mongoose
Ichneumia albicauda

Length of the Body: about 20 inches
Length of the Tail: about 16 inches
Weight: about 11 pounds
Diet: mainly insects

Number of Young: 1 to 3
Home: Africa and southern Arabia
Order: Carnivores
Family: Viverrids, aardwolves, and hyenas

 Grasslands

 Mammals

African visitors on safari often see the large white-tailed mongoose standing in the light of their vehicles. This mongoose is one of the most common and widespread of its kind. It is most numerous on Africa's tree-dotted savannas.

Weighing about 11 pounds, the whitetail is one of the largest mongooses. It is distinguished by its long, thickly furred tail, which is much lighter than its grayish-brown body. Its legs are dark brown to black, and considerably longer than those of other mongooses. But like its cousins, the white-tailed mongoose has a long body; coarse, dull-colored fur; and strong digging claws.

In the dark of night, this solitary hunter catches small animals and feeds on ripe fruits. It is even able to crack open eggs. Holding an egg in its front paws, the mongoose may throw the egg through its back legs, like a football player "hiking a ball." Or it may simply drop the egg to the ground from a standing-upright position.

This intelligent animal even "dances" in front of chicken pens. When a hen sticks the top of its body through the fence to watch the show, the mongoose bites off the hen's head. Obviously, such trickery has made enemies among many farmers. Outside of raiding henhouses, the shy and solitary white-tailed mongoose avoids civilization. During the day, it retreats to a cave or to a den beneath a tree.

Cape Monitor
Varanus exanthematicus albigularis

Length: up to 5 feet
Weight: up to 20 pounds
Diet: eggs, small and medium-size animals, and carcasses
Method of Reproduction: egg layer

Home: southern Africa
Order: Lizards and snakes
Family: Monitor lizards

 Grasslands

 Reptiles

© AUSTIN J. STEVENS / ANIMALS ANIMALS / EARTH SCENES

The Cape monitor belongs to a family of very large lizards. Its cousins include the largest lizard of all: the 9-foot-long Komodo dragon, *Varanus komodoensis*, of Indonesia. The Cape monitor is also a heavyweight, with muscular legs and powerful claws on each of its five-toed feet. Its head is large and pointed, and its neck is long. The monitor's powerful tail is nearly twice the length of its body.

The Cape monitor lives on Africa's lightly wooded grasslands. There each adult male tries to defend a territory of up to 25 square miles. When they fight, the males stand up on their hind legs, face-to-face. Then each tries to push the other over.

Usually the strongest proves his point before either combatant is harmed. Although their teeth are sharp, the monitors rarely bite each other. But they will resort to biting when threatened by a predator or a human. They have been known to break the bones of humans by lashing out with their heavy tail.

Within his territory a male monitor may travel several miles a day. As he patrols his borders, he searches for food (eggs, small animals, and carcasses) and potential mates. During mating the male clasps his front legs around the back legs of the female and tickles her neck by flicking his tongue. Later she lays her eggs in a tree hollow or in a termite mound.

Desert Monitor
Varanus griseus

Length of the Body: 5 feet
Length of the Tail: 4 feet
Diet: small mammals, reptiles, and eggs
Number of Young: 20

Home: North Africa and the Middle East
Order: Lizards
Family: Monitor lizards

 Deserts

Reptiles

© BIOS / PETER ARNOLD, INC.

Endangered Animals

The desert monitor is quite unlike its more famous cousin, the Komodo dragon. The exotic Komodo lives in the lush rainforest where it can feast on water buffalo and deer. The desert monitor is born to a harsher life. Its home is the Sahara and other dry deserts of the Middle East.

Fortunately, the desert monitor is designed to survive in parched surroundings. Since food is scarce in the desert, this monitor can go months between meals and almost as long without water. When a sudden downpour does arrive, the lizard is ready. It can suck in huge amounts of water—as much as 15 percent of its own weight. For comparison, this would be like a full-grown man drinking 3 gallons of water at once! The desert monitor also works hard to stay cool. It does most of its hunting well before dawn. And it digs holes throughout its home territory, where it can hide from the hot desert sun.

Thanks to its intimidating size, the desert monitor has few natural enemies. If challenged, however, it puts up a frightening fight. It can puff up its neck to look even larger and scarier than normal. The desert monitor also has a powerful weapon in its long tail, which it can whip about like a sharp, scaly sword. Despite its fearsome defenses, the desert monitor is in danger of extinction. It have been overhunted for its unusual skin.

Gould's Monitor
Varanus gouldii

Length: 4 feet
Number of Eggs: 11
Home: Australia and New
  Guinea

Diet: insects and lizards
Order: Lizards and snakes
Family: Monitor lizards

 Deserts

 Reptiles

© JIM HANKEN / BRUCE COLEMAN INC.

In the wide-open spaces of Australia, it's common to see a Gould's monitor running at full speed on its hind legs. It looks like a monster from a science-fiction movie! It's nicknamed the "monitor racehorse" because of its speed. Even though it is scary-looking, the monitor does not attack humans, but it will defend itself if attacked. Standing on its hind legs, it puffs out its neck to frighten its enemy. If cornered, it can strike violent blows with its tail and claws, sometimes causing serious injury.

Usually, the monitor dashes around the desert, looking for prey. It can cover a huge area, chasing small lizards, snakes, and insects. When it catches prey, the monitor grabs it and hits it hard against the ground.

It can swallow large prey because it has an expandable throat. If the prey is too big, it rips the animal apart with its claws and teeth before eating it. The Gould's monitor sometimes raids chicken coops, stealing eggs and even chickens. Because of this, and also because it is considered to be a delicious food, the monitor has been hunted widely. All the same, it is still the most common lizard in Australia. Its brown body, spotted with yellow, makes it almost impossible to see because it blends in with the sandy soil in the area where it lives. There are three different types of Gould's monitor; each type has a slightly different color, but they all have large black stripes next to their eyes.

Nile Monitor
Varanus niloticus

Length: 39 to 84 inches
Weight: 10 to 50 pounds
Diet: reptile eggs, fish, and crabs
Number of Eggs: 29 to 60

Home: sub-Saharan Africa
Order: Lizards and snakes
Family: Monitor lizards
Subclass: Scaly reptiles
Suborder: Lizards

 Fresh Water

 Reptiles

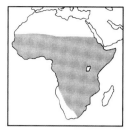

© P. DREINERT / OKAPIA / PHOTO RESEARCHERS

At 6½ feet, the Nile monitor is the longest lizard in all of Africa. With its muscular legs and long, sharp claws, the creature can be a frightening sight. For the most part, however, it prefers to be a gentle giant. When bothered, it will usually dive into the water to escape. But if cornered, this lizard will fight to the death! The Nile monitor can bite, slash with its claws, and strike enemies with its powerful, broad tail.

Monitors are cold-blooded animals and must warm their bodies in the sun. In the morning the Nile monitor lies on a rock or a little island of sun in the river. When the sun's warmth has penetrated its body, the Nile monitor is ready to dive into the water

in search of food. Its strong forearms make it a good swimmer. It uses its flattened tail to steer, like a rudder on a boat.

Only the female ventures far from water, and then only to search for a termite mound. Once she finds the perfect spot, she tears apart the mound with her powerful front legs and claws. When she reaches the center of the nest, she lays as many as 60 eggs. The frantic termites quickly rebuild their home, surrounding the eggs with dried mud. There the eggs remain, warm and well protected, for four to six months. The baby monitors must wait until the summer rains soften the hard termite mound. Then they claw their way out, leaving the termites with another mess to clean up!

Goeldi's Monkey
Callimico goeldii

Length of the Body: 9 inches
Length of the Tail: 11 inches
Weight: 1.1 pounds
Diet: mainly fruits and insects
Number of Young: 1

Home: upper Amazon River Basin of South America
Order: Primates
Family: Goeldi's monkey

 Forests and Mountains

Mammals

© ROD WILLIAMS / BRUCE COLEMAN INC.

? Endangered Animals

Goeldi's monkeys communicate among themselves using sounds and gestures. While traveling through the forest, they keep in touch through loud cries. They even "talk" softly when sitting side by side. If a monkey senses danger, it raises the fur on its back and lets out a loud warning "chuck." And, like people, Goeldi's monkeys use a variety of body gestures—including stares, frowns, and hand movements—to express ideas.

A shy animal, Goeldi's monkey is small, black, and seldom seen in the wild. It makes its home in forests among dense shrubs and other low-growing plants. Powerful legs enable the creature to make long leaps and to cling onto tree trunks, using all four feet to hold on. To jump from tree to tree, this acrobatic primate pushes off backward and turns in midair so that, upon landing, it can readily grab the second tree trunk.

Goeldi's monkeys live in small family groups of 4 to 10 individuals. Each group has its own territory and spends a typical day traveling, eating, and resting. The group moves from tree to tree in search of ripe fruit. In the trees or on the ground in between, the monkeys also find tasty insects and frogs, lizards, and other small invertebrates to eat. Goeldi's monkeys usually take three rest breaks during the day to sunbathe or groom one another. After such a busy day, the group sleeps the night away among the bushes or in a hollow tree.

Savanna Monkey (Grivet)
Cercopithecus aethiops

Length of the Body: up to 24 inches
Length of the Tail: up to 35 inches
Diet: mainly plant matter; also some invertebrates

Weight: 6 to 15 pounds
Number of Young: 1
Home: sub-Saharan Africa
Order: Primates
Family: Old World monkeys

 Grasslands

 Mammals

© JOE MCDONALD / BRUCE COLEMAN INC.

Most anyone who has gone on a safari has seen a savanna monkey, a black-faced creature with white tufts of hair on its cheeks and a white band of hair on its forehead. Those monkeys living in national parks aren't afraid of people. They are curious animals, hopping onto automobiles and wandering onto hotel grounds to see if there's anything tasty for them to eat. Despite their apparent abundance along safari routes, most savanna monkeys live on savannas near the edge of woodlands. They are mainly vegetarians, feeding on grass, leaves, fruit, and other plant matter.

Savanna monkeys usually live in bands of 6 to 20 individuals. They have many enemies, including leopards, baboons, hyenas, eagles, pythons, and crocodiles. The monkey relies on its good eyesight and quick escape abilities for defense. For example, when a leopard appears, the monkey runs into the woods and climbs into the treetops. When an eagle attacks, the monkey rushes to hide among dense bushes. When one member of a band sees an enemy, it cries to warn the other monkeys in the band. Different cries are used to warn of leopards, birds of prey, and snakes.

Adult males are bigger than females. At birth a baby weighs 11 to 14 ounces. It depends on its mother for milk until it is about six months old. The life span of the savanna monkey is more than 30 years.

Woolly Spider Monkey (Muriqui)
Brachyteles arachnoides

Length of the Body: 18 to 25 inches
Length of the Tail: 2¼ to 2¾ feet
Diet: mainly leaves; also fruits, seeds, berries, and flowers

Weight: about 20 pounds
Number of Young: 1
Home: southeastern Brazil
Order: Primates
Family: Capuchinlike monkeys

  Rainforests

 Mammals

© KEVIN SCHAFER / CORBIS

? Endangered Animals

In Brazil the woolly spider monkey is known by the native name *muriqui*. It is the largest primate in the Americas. Unfortunately, it is also the closest to extinction. As few as 300 individuals remain, and they are scattered over hundreds of miles of rainforest. Only the strict protection of their habitat will save this rare monkey. There is hope: a family of cattle ranchers in São Paulo has preserved about 7,500 acres of undisturbed rainforest for the species. At last report, there were about 85 woolly spider monkeys living in patches of this forest.

In many ways, this primate looks like a cross between its two cousins, the woolly monkey and the spider monkey. Like a woolly monkey, it has a sturdy body and soft, woolly fur. It can swing through the trees, hand over hand, like a true spider monkey. And like a spider monkey, it has a long, strong tail, which it uses like an extra hand.

Woolly spider monkeys live in large, loosely knit families. Usually these family groups separate into smaller units that forage for food on their own. One subgroup may be all-female and another all-male, but youngsters always stay with their mothers. When a female is fertile, she uses a special call to announce her readiness to mate. In response to the female's cries, the males in the area gather around and follow her through the trees for several days until one of the males mates with her.

Gila Monster
Heloderma suspectum

Length: up to 23 inches
Weight: up to 3¼ pounds
Diet: rodents, rabbits, and birds
Number of Young: 3 to 15

Home: northern United States and southwestern Mexico
Order: Lizards and snakes
Family: Poisonous lizards

 Deserts

 Reptiles

© DAVID A. NORTHCOTT / CORBIS

There are more than 3,000 kinds of lizards in the world. Of all those, only two—the Gila monster and its close relative, the beaded lizard—are poisonous. The Gila monster uses its poison for defense, not for catching food. Its venom can kill small animals, but it rarely kills a person. Gila monsters will not attack people unless they are provoked. When provoked, they hiss, just like their cousins, the snakes.

Gila monsters live in the deserts of the southwestern United States and northern Mexico. They were named after the Gila River basin in Arizona, where Spanish explorers first saw them hundreds of years ago. They are most active during the rainy season. During the heat of the day, they lie in the shade or under the sand. They come out at night to look for food. Gila monsters eat bird and reptile eggs, birds, and other small animals. They are slow-moving, except when they spot something to eat. Then they dart quickly with their powerful legs. Their jaws and teeth are very strong, and they clamp on to their prey until it dies. Gila monsters can go without eating for many months.

Gila monsters mate during the summer. The female digs a shallow hole in the sand, lays her eggs there, and covers them with sand. The eggs hatch in about a month. There are usually between 3 and 15 offspring.

Eastern Malaria Mosquito
Anopheles quadrimaculatus

Diet of the Male: plant fluids
Diet of the Female: plant fluids and blood
Method of Reproduction: egg layer

Length: about ⅕ inch
Home: eastern United States and Central America
Order: Flies
Family: Mosquitoes

  Fresh Water

Arthropods

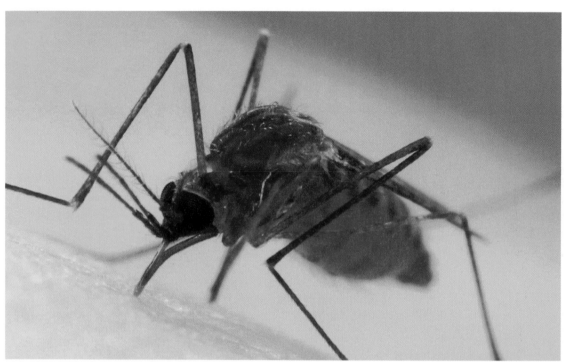

© DARLYNE A. MURAWSKI / PETER ARNOLD, INC.

The word "mosquito" comes from the Spanish word for "little fly." The eastern malaria mosquito also takes part of its name from the deadly disease that the female spreads. There are more than 2,700 species of mosquitoes in the world. Fortunately, few of them carry malaria, an often fatal disease. The common mosquitoes of North America, for example, do not carry the disease.

Though once abundant, the eastern-malaria-mosquito population has been greatly reduced. People have worked hard to stop its deadly spread—either by eliminating the watery places where it breeds or by spraying pesticides.

Like all mosquitoes, the eastern malaria mosquito has a long, needle-like sucking device on its mouth. The male uses this device, called a *proboscis*, only to suck plant juices. The female, however, needs a blood meal in order to produce yolk for her eggs. It is during this blood sucking that the malaria mosquito transmits her disease. The direct cause of malaria is a one-celled animal called a *plasmodium*. The mosquito carries the plasmodium from one person to another. The plasmodium does not merely hitch a ride on the mosquito, though. It must also be able to reproduce while it is in the mosquito's body. Plasmodia can do this only in certain species of mosquito such as the eastern malaria variety.

Common Magpie Moth
Abraxas grossulariata

Diet of the Caterpillar: leaves of fruit trees and berry bushes
Method of Reproduction: egg layer

Wingspan: 1½ to 1¾ inches
Home: Eurasia
Order: Butterflies and moths
Family: Geometrid moths

 Forests and Mountains

Arthropods

© ANNIE POOLE / PAPILIO / CORBIS

The common magpie moth, like the bird for which it is named, is boldly marked in black and white. Magpie moths are infamous across Europe because their caterpillars severely damage the leaves of fruit trees and berry bushes.

When it hatches, the magpie larva is less than ¹⁄₁₀th of an inch. Its tiny body is yellowish orange with a black head. The larva spends most of its first summer hanging from a leaf on a silken thread. After sleeping through the winter, it becomes active again in spring. Magpie caterpillars feed on the leaves of various trees and shrubs. They do their greatest damage to gooseberry and currant bushes.

When full-grown, the magpie caterpillar has a white body with black spots and a reddish-orange "racing" stripe. If disturbed, the caterpillar falls to the ground and curls up in a tight "U" shape, as if dead. In June the caterpillar hangs from a leaf, stem, or fence and encloses itself in a flimsy, transparent cocoon. The adult moth hatches about three weeks later.

Like many moths, magpies fly at night and are attracted to lights. Male magpies have feathery antennae, which help them pick up the scent of their mates. The female lays batches of creamy-white eggs under the leaves of plants. The eggs turn a bluish black before hatching two to three weeks later.

Six-spot Burnet Moth
Zygaena filipendulae

Wingspan: up to 1½ inches
Diet: nectar (adult); leaves (larva)
Method of Reproduction: egg layer

Home: Europe and western Asia
Order: Butterflies and moths
Family: Burnet moths

 Grasslands

 Arthropods

© IFA / PETER ARNOLD, INC.

It's tough to miss a six-spot moth as it flutters through a field. The bright red spots on its front wings and its red back wings make it very conspicuous. Despite its flashy colors, birds and other predators seldom try to catch burnet moths. In fact, a bird that catches and tries to eat one of these moths quickly learns an important lesson: burnet moths taste awful! They also secrete a poisonous liquid. Their bright colors warn predators to "keep off."

Burnets are small moths with a thick body and two long antennae on the head that thicken near the tip. Burnets are active during the daytime, especially when the sun is shining. They fly slowly through

meadows and across bush-covered hillsides, traveling from one flower to the next. They use their long, tubelike tongue to sip nectar from the center of flowers. Burnet moths' favorite food plants include thistles and mourning brides.

Female burnet moths lay their eggs in early summer. The eggs hatch into caterpillars in late summer. The caterpillars feed on leaves until cold weather comes. Then the caterpillars hibernate through the winter. The following spring, they enter the pupal stage when they settle on a plant stem and spin a silken cocoon around themselves. During the pupal stage the insects change, or metamorphose, into adults.

European Mouflon
Ovis ammon musimon

Height at the Shoulder: up to 3⅓ feet
Number of Young: usually 1
Home: native to Sardinia and Corsica; introduced to central Europe, Texas, and Hawaii

Length: about 5 feet
Weight: up to 200 pounds
Diet: plant matter
Order: Even-toed hoofed mammals
Family: Bovines

Forests and Mountains

Mammals

© MAGNUS NYMAN / NATURE PICTURE LIBRARY

Originally the European mouflon ranged only through the hilly mountains of Sardinia and Corsica, two large islands off the western coast of Italy. In the past century, however, these small wild sheep were introduced to the forests of central Europe. Ranchers have also imported mouflons to Texas and Hawaii, and interbred them with domestic sheep.

The mouflon ram is famous for his large, curling horns, which are even larger than those of the American bighorn sheep. The female mouflon has smaller horns. The mouflon ram is also recognized by a pale, saddle-shaped patch across his back and flanks.

During most of the year, the rams and does live in separate herds. As the breeding, or "rutting," season begins, the rams engage in violent duels. They kick and sideswipe each other and charge head-on, crashing their massive horns together. The strongest rams win the right to mate with the members of a female herd. Five months later, each mated female gives birth to a single lamb. Twins are a rarity among European mouflons, although common among their Asian cousins.

Aside from hunters the mouflon's enemies include wolves and bears. Females must also guard their young from prowling foxes and eagles. The mouflon's best defenses are its keen eyesight and great speed.

Egyptian Spiny Mouse
Acomys cahirinus

Length of the Body: 5 inches
Length of the Tail: 5 inches
Weight: 2 to 3 ounces
Diet: mostly seeds; occasionally worms and insects

Number of Young: usually 2 or 3
Home: northern Egypt
Order: Rodents
Family: Rats and mice

 Deserts

 Mammals

© ERWIN AND PEGGY BAUER / BRUCE COLEMAN INC.

The Egyptian spiny mouse gets its name from the hard, bristly hairs in its outer coat. These dark-colored "spines" grow only on the mouse's back; its belly is covered with a silky white down.

In cities and towns, the Egyptian spiny mouse lives a life very similar to that of the familiar house mouse, *Mus musculus*. It steals grain and bread from kitchens, and builds its nest in the corner of a basement or behind a hollow wall. In the African desert, the Egyptian spiny mouse lives a life very similar to that of a gerbil. In fact, families of Egyptian spiny mice sometimes take over gerbil burrows when their "homeowners" are away.

While other species of mice give birth to blind, helpless babies, the spiny mouse comes into the world with its eyes open. Within three days the newborn can already toddle around on shaky legs. The baby grows so quickly that the mother spiny mouse doesn't even bother to build a proper nest. In about three months, the young are old enough to have babies of their own.

The Egyptian spiny mouse hunts for its food in the morning and late afternoon. It takes a long nap at midday to avoid the heat of the North African sun. Like many desert animals, this mouse has large, hairless ears. This helps the animal stay cool by exposing many blood vessels to the air.

Wood Mouse
Apodemus sylvaticus

Length of the Body: 3¼ to 4¼ inches

Length of the Tail: 2¾ to 4½ inches

Diet: seeds, fruits, insects, and snails

Weight: ⅔ to 1 ounce

Number of Young: 4 to 7

Home: Europe and northern Africa

Order: Rodents

Family: True mice

 Forests and Mountains

 Mammals

© NEIL MILLER / PAPILIO / CORBIS

Like a summer camper eager to return home, the wood mouse comes in from the outdoors in fall. Leaving forest, field, or orchard, it moves into farmhouses or rural cottages. There the wintering wood mouse often helps itself to the homeowner's grain and fruit. Then, in the spring, the mouse scampers outdoors again, eager to camp among the thick grass and weeds. In the wild the wood mouse spends most of its time on the ground, plucking fruit and seeds from herbs and small bushes.

Some people call this little rodent the jumping mouse. It has a habit of fleeing from danger by hopping on its back legs. The wood mouse is also a good climber and sometimes hunts for berries and fruit in the treetops. It has even been seen gliding from branch to branch and tree to tree.

The wood mouse has a closely related twin, the yellow-necked mouse. Even scientists have a hard time telling the two species apart. Both are shiny brown mice with very large eyes and ears. These features help the mice sense the approach of enemies in the dark of night, which is when the mice are most active. In order to coexist peacefully in the same area, wood mice and yellow-necked mice avoid one another. Wood mice stay among grass and weeds, while their cousins live in trees and shrubs. But if you were to lock the two in a cage, you would soon see which is stronger. Yellow-necked mice will chase and even kill wood mice.

Swan Mussel
Anodonta cygnaea

Length: 6 to 9 inches
Diet: plankton
Method of Reproduction:
    live-bearer

Home: Europe
Order: Freshwater mussels
Family: River mussels

 Fresh Water

Other
Invertebrates

© PAUL HOBSON / NATURE PICTURE LIBRARY

A delicate, frilly tube, or siphon, peeks from one side of the swan mussel's thin, oval shell. With this tube, the swan mussel sucks down more than 18 gallons of water a day! It expels the water through a second tube. But first the mussel must filter oxygen and food from the water, using its gills.

Adult swan mussels live in the sand and gravel of freshwater streams. They root themselves securely to the ground using a strong muscular foot. After breeding, the female swan mussel keeps her fertile eggs inside her gills. When the eggs hatch, the mussel blows newborn larvae out through the second siphon.

The swan mussel's larvae, or immature young, are fascinating creatures that don't much resemble their parents. Under a microscope, these larvae (called glochidia) look like tiny clams with two enormous teeth at the front of their gaping shell. The glochidia use their tiny, sharp teeth to attach to the skin or gills of fish. There they feed on blood and tissue. A fish may have up to 3,000 glochidia parasites attached to its body! When they've eaten their fill, the glochidia drop off, settle to the bottom of the stream, and transform into adult swan mussels.

The swan mussel is one of the largest of the freshwater bivalves. Pollutants easily poison it, however. So it doesn't survive in contaminated waters.

40

Narwhal
Monodon monoceros

Length: 14 to 21 feet
Weight: 1,760 to 3,960 pounds
Number of Young: 1
Home: Arctic Ocean and northern Atlantic and Pacific oceans

Diet: squid, flounder, and other bottom-dwelling fish
Order: Whales, dolphins, and porpoises
Family: Narwhals and belugas
Suborder: Toothed whales

 Oceans and Shores

 Mammals

© FLIP NICKLIN / MINDEN PICTURES

In medieval times, people believed that the narwhal's 6-foot-long "horn" held magical and medicinal powers. Its ivory spike was literally worth its weight in gold. As a result, horn-hunting sailors traveled to the Arctic and slaughtered "sea unicorns" by the tens of thousands. Even today, souvenir hunters kill narwhals solely for their spiral horns, which are carved into ivory jewelry.

Narwhals have two teeth. In the female, both teeth stay hidden in her jawbone. In the male the left tooth grows into an enormous pointed lance. The largest narwhal tusk ever found was more than 8 feet long!

Scientists once thought that male narwhals used their long spears to duel with one another or to break holes in the Arctic ice. In truth the narwhal's tusk is too brittle to be used for fighting or chiseling. Most likely the male uses it to impress female narwhals.

Narwhals love cold ocean water, and nowhere is it colder than in the Arctic! These whales spend most of their lives swimming beneath huge floes of ice that stretch for miles in every direction. As they travel, narwhals look for holes in the ice above their head. Like all whales, they need to breathe air. But surfacing at a breathing hole can be dangerous in the Arctic. Killer polar bears often wait in ambush on the ice above.

Sea Nettle
Chrysaora quinquecirrha

Method of Reproduction: egg layer
Home: Gulf of Mexico and western Atlantic Ocean from Cape Cod to Florida

Width: 8 to 10 inches
Diet: mainly small fish
Order: Semaestomids
Family: Pelagids

Oceans and Shores

Other Invertebrates

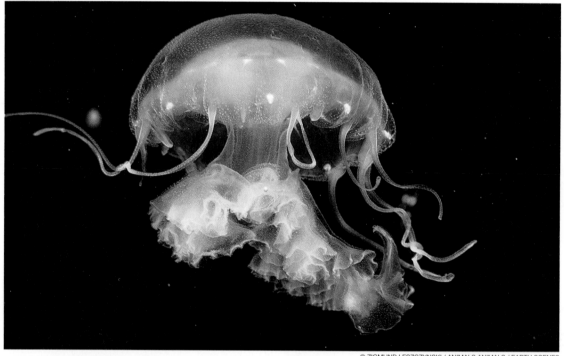

© ZIGMUND LESZCZYNSKI / ANIMALS ANIMALS / EARTH SCENES

Floating lazily near the water's surface, the beautiful sea nettle looks like a sea fairy dressed in many layers of pink taffeta. But beware of this beauty! Touching it is like grasping a stinging nettle plant. Even a slight brush with this moderately toxic jellyfish produces an itchy red rash. Yet a direct sting can be very painful—serious enough to warrant an immediate trip to the emergency room.

The sea nettle often washes up on beaches along the Eastern Seaboard of the United States. It is especially common in Chesapeake Bay in the mid-Atlantic states. Its cousin, the lined sea nettle, occasionally appears on western beaches from Alaska to Southern California.

The sea nettle's partly transparent umbrella, or "bell," is decorated with red dots and stripes, and many wartlike bumps. The bell carries 40 long golden tentacles. In between each tentacle are sensitive lobes that the creature uses to "smell" the water for any traces of prey. Beneath the circle of tentacles are four long pink ruffles. These are the sea nettle's "lips," and they form a type of feeding tube. They also carry the creature's stinging cells. Like other true jellyfish, the sea nettle swims slowly and rhythmically by contracting and relaxing its bell.

Alpine Newt
Triturus alpestris

Length: 2¾ to 4½ inches
Diet: small crustaceans, insects and their larvae, and worms
Home: Central and southern Europe

Number of Eggs: about 150
Order: Salamanders and newts
Family: Newts and their relatives

 Fresh Water

 Amphibians

© RENE KREKELS / FOTO NATURA / MINDEN PICTURES

Alpine newts are most common in mountain habitats of Central and southern Europe at elevations as high as 9,000 feet. But they're not too picky about where they live. They also inhabit low-lying areas, making homes in lakes, ponds, swamps, and slow-moving streams. Usually they stay near the bottom of the water and do not swim about. Occasionally alpine newts will wander onto land, where they live under rocks and tree roots. Populations of alpine newts have dropped in many parts of their range. People have introduced trout and other game fish into lakes where the newts live. These fish have eaten almost all the newts, and newts are now quite rare in some areas.

The alpine newt has a bright orange-red belly. During most of the year, its back is gray-black. Then, at the beginning of the breeding season, the back turns bluish. The male develops a yellowish crest spotted with black on its back. Alpine newts breed in late winter or early spring, depending on the altitude. Newts that live high in the mountains breed later than newts that live in lower habitats.

Alpine newts breed in small bodies of water where they can hide among plants. The female attaches her eggs—either singly or in small groups—to an underwater plant. In two or four weeks, depending on the water temperature, the eggs hatch into dark-gray larvae. A larva is only 5/16 inch long upon hatching, but it grows fast. The larval stage usually lasts three to four months, but it can last as long as two years.

Crested (Warty) Newt
Triturus cristatus

Diet: worms, slugs, snails, insects, and insect larvae
Method of Reproduction: egg layer
Home: Europe and western Asia

Length: 5 to 7 inches
Order: Salamanders and newts
Family: Newts and their relatives

Fresh Water

Amphibians

© GEORGE MCCARTHY / CORBIS

Crested newts spend much of the year on land. During the day, they hide under stones or among thick grasses. At night, especially when it is raining or very humid, they crawl about in search of worms and other prey, which they seize in their jaws. In colder parts of their range, they usually hibernate through the winter. Spring and early summer are the breeding seasons for crested newts. During this time the creatures live in ponds and swamps, spending much of the time underwater. Every so often, they swim to the surface for a gulp of fresh air. Then they quickly return to the bottom.

During the breeding season, the newts undergo remarkable changes. A high crest develops along the male's back, from its head almost to the end of its tail. The female develops tail ridges, and the male grows a long tail fin. The males also change their coloring. The skin on their body and tail turns light olive green, with many black spots. The males court the females with elaborate and enthusiastic dances, displaying their crests and coloration. After mating, the females lay one egg at a time. They carefully attach each egg to a leaf of a plant in the water, then fold the leaf over to hide the egg. Each female lays 200 to 300 eggs during the breeding season. The eggs hatch into tiny, slender larvae. The larvae grow rapidly, and about four months after hatching, they are ready to leave the water and begin their adult life on land.

Set Index

A

adder **1:**5
adder, rhombic night **1:**6
African bat-eared fox **3:**42
African scorpion, giant **8:**16
African snail, giant **8:**37
African twig snake **8:**38
African wild dog **3:**20
agile frog **3:**44
agouti, orange-rumped **1:**7
Alaskan pika (collared pika) **7:**23
Algerian hedgehog **5:**11
alligator lizard, southern **5:**41
alpaca **1:**8
alpine newt **6:**43
American black vulture **10:**24
American crow **3:**8
American tree sparrow **9:**11
amphibians
    caecilian, Ceylonese **2:**10
    frog, agile **3:**44
    frog, burrowing tree **4:**5
    frog, common gray tree **4:**6
    frog, European tree **4:**7
    frog, gold **4:**8
    frog, marbled reed **4:**9
    frog, marsupial **4:**10
    frog, moor **4:**11
    frog, northern chorus **4:**12
    frog, ornate horned **4:**13
    frog, paradox **4:**14
    frog, pickerel **4:**15
    frog, pig **4:**16
    frog, red-legged **4:**17
    frog, strawberry poison dart
      4:18
    newt, alpine **6:**43
    newt, crested (warty) **6:**44
    salamander, common dusky
      8:13
    salamander, fire **8:**14
    spadefoot, European **9:**10
    toad, Eurasian common **9:**42
    toad, green **9:**43
    toad, Surinam **9:**44
anemone, opelet **1:**9
anemone, silver-spotted (gem
    anemone) **1:**10
angel shark, European **8:**22
anoa **1:**11
ant, leaf-cutter **1:**12
anteater, dwarf **1:**13
anteater, scaly (giant pangolin)
    1:14
arctic fulmar **4:**19
arctic hare **5:**7
argus, blue-spotted **1:**15
arrau (giant South American river
    turtle) **10:**14
arthropods **6:**18
    ant, leaf-cutter **1:**12
    backswimmer, common **1:**16
    beetle, cellar **1:**28
    beetle, checkered (bee-wolf)
      1:29
    beetle, European rhinoceros
      1:30
    beetle, forest dung **1:**31
    beetle, whirligig **1:**32
    butterfly, brimstone **2:**7
    butterfly, sail (scarce
      swallowtail) **2:**8
    cockroach, wood **2:**32
    cricket, bush (bush katydid)
      2:44
    cricket, European mole **3:**5
    cricket, Mormon **3:**6
    daphnia (water flea) **3:**37
    darner, blue-green **3:**12
    darner, green **3:**13
    fly, large bee **3:**40
    grasshopper, blue-winged
      wasteland **4:**36
    grasshopper, green valley **4:**37
    hawkmoth, broad-bordered bee
      5:10

horntail, large **5:**17
horsefly, cattle **5:**19
katydid, steppe **5:**26
locust, migratory **6:**5
louse, human-body **6:**7
mosquito, eastern malaria **6:**34
moth, common magpie **6:**35
moth, six-spot burnet **6:**36
prawn, common European
    (palaemon) **7:**33
scorpion, giant African **8:**16
sexton (burying beetle) **8:**20
snakefly **9:**5
spider, goldenrod **9:**14
swallowtail, common
    European **9:**29
tortoiseshell **10:**7
treehopper **10:**9
treehopper, oak **10:**10
white, marbled **10:**36
Atlantic cod **2:**33
Australian lungfish **6:**8
Australian sea lion **8:**17
axis deer (chital) **3:**14
azure-winged magpie **6:**13

B

backswimmer, common **1:**16
Baikal seal **8:**18
Baird's beaked whale **10:**34
bandicoot, large, short-nosed **1:**17
barb, half-banded **1:**18
barbet, crimson-breasted **1:**19
barnacle, common goose **1:**20
barracuda, Pacific **1:**21
basilisk, double-crested **1:**22
bat, Gambian epaulet **1:**23
bat, Honduran white **1:**24
bat, large mouse-eared **1:**25
bat-eared fox, African **3:**42
beaked whale, Baird's **10:**34
bear, sloth **1:**26
bearded vulture **10:**25
beaver, Eurasian **1:**27
bee fly, large **3:**40
bee hawkmoth, broad-bordered
    5:10
beetle, burying (sexton) **8:**20
beetle, cellar **1:**28
beetle, checkered (bee-wolf) **1:**29
beetle, European rhinoceros **1:**30
beetle, forest dung **1:**31
beetle, whirligig **1:**32
bee-wolf (checkered beetle) **1:**29
bird of paradise, greater **1:**33
birds
    barbet, crimson-breasted **1:**19
    bird of paradise, greater **1:**33
    bittern, Eurasian **1:**35
    bluebird, blue-backed fairy
      1:37
    booby, blue-footed **1:**38
    booby, brown **1:**39
    bower-bird, satin **1:**40
    bunting, corn **2:**5
    chickadee, black-capped **2:**23
    chicken, greater prairie **2:**24
    courser, cream-colored **2:**43
    crossbill, red **3:**7
    crow, American **3:**8
    crow, carrion **3:**9
    crow, fish **3:**10
    dove, laughing **3:**24
    duck, torrent **3:**26
    dunlin **3:**27
    eagle, tawny **3:**30
    finch, snow **3:**36
    flicker, red-shafted **3:**38
    flycatcher, fork-tailed **3:**41
    fulmar, arctic **4:**19
    goose, magpie **4:**33
    greenfinch **4:**38
    greenshank **4:**39
    grouse, double-banded sand
      4:40
    gull, great black-backed **5:**5

heron, little blue **5:**12
heron, nankeen night **5:**13
heron, purple **5:**14
hornbill, red-billed **5:**16
jacamar, rufous-tailed **5:**21
jacana, wattled **5:**22
lapwing **5:**31
lorikeet, musk **6:**6
macaw, blue-and-yellow **6:**11
macaw, military **6:**12
magpie, azure-winged **6:**13
manakin, red-capped **6:**15
martin, sand **6:**17
merganser, red-breasted **6:**19
nuthatch, Eurasian **7:**5
owl, great gray **7:**8
owl, scops **7:**9
owl, short-eared **7:**10
owl, tawny **7:**11
parakeet, rose-ringed **7:**13
parrot, king **7:**14
penguin, Galápagos **7:**16
penguin, gentoo **7:**17
petrel, southern giant **7:**19
pheasant, Reeve's **7:**20
pipit, water **7:**24
plover, spur-winged **7:**26
pochard, red-crested **7:**27
puffin, tufted **7:**35
quail, little button **7:**40
quetzal **7:**41
roller, common **8:**9
roller, lilac-breasted **8:**10
sandpiper, wood **8:**15
shag, imperial **8:**21
shelduck, common **8:**26
siskin, Eurasian **8:**30
sparrow, American tree **9:**11
sparrow, hedge **9:**12
sparrow, Java **9:**13
starling, superb **9:**22
stonechat **9:**24
stork, white **9:**25
swan, whooper **9:**30
tanager, scarlet **9:**33
tern, whiskered **9:**37
thrush, mistle **9:**40
thrush, rock **9:**41
toucan, keel-billed **10:**8
vireo, white-eyed **10:**21
vulture, American black **10:**24
vulture, bearded **10:**25
vulture, king **10:**26
vulture, lappet-faced **10:**27
wagtail, white **10:**28
wagtail, yellow **10:**29
waxbill, red-cheeked (cordon-
    bleu) **10:**30
waxwing, cedar **10:**31
weaver, grenadier (red bishop)
    10:32
whydah, pin-tailed **10:**37
wren, superb blue **10:**43
bishop, red (grenadier weaver)
    10:32
bitterling **1:**34
bittern, Eurasian **1:**35
black-backed gull, great **5:**5
black-backed jackal **5:**23
blackbuck **1:**36
black-capped chickadee **2:**23
black mamba **6:**14
black ruby **8:**11
black vulture, American **10:**24
bleeding-heart tetra **9:**38
blind cavefish **2:**20
blue-and-yellow macaw **6:**11
blue-backed fairy bluebird **1:**37
bluebird, blue-backed fairy **1:**37
blue-footed booby **1:**38
blue-green darner **3:**12
blue heron, little **5:**12
blue-spotted argus **1:**15
blue stentor **9:**23
blue-tailed day gecko **4:**24
blue-winged wasteland
    grasshopper **4:**36

blue wren, superb **10:**43
booby, blue-footed **1:**38
booby, brown **1:**39
bower-bird, satin **1:**40
bowfin **1:**41
bream, common **1:**42
brimstone butterfly **2:**7
broad-bordered bee hawkmoth
    5:10
brocket, red **1:**43
bronze catfish **2:**16
brown booby **1:**39
brush-tailed possum **7:**31
buffalo, water **1:**44
bunting, corn **2:**5
burnet moth, six-spot **6:**36
burrowing tree frog **4:**5
burying beetle (sexton) **8:**20
bushbuck **2:**6
bush cricket (bush katydid) **2:**44
butterfly, brimstone **2:**7
butterfly, sail (scarce swallowtail)
    2:8
butterflyfish, freshwater **2:**9
button quail, little **7:**40

C

caecilian, Ceylonese **2:**10
California legless lizard **5:**33
Cape girdled lizard, common
    5:34
Cape hyrax **5:**20
Cape monitor **6:**26
caribou (reindeer) **8:**7
carp, common **2:**11
carpet python **7:**36
carpet shell, crosscut **8:**27
carrion crow **3:**9
cat, European wild **2:**12
cat, Geoffroy's **2:**13
cat, Iriomote **2:**14
cat, ring-tailed **2:**15
catfish, bronze **2:**16
catfish, Congo **2:**17
catfish, glass **2:**18
catfish, shovelnose **2:**19
cat tapeworm **9:**34
cavefish, blind **2:**20
cedar waxwing **10:**31
cellar beetle **1:**28
Ceylonese caecilian **2:**10
chamois **2:**21
checkered beetle (bee-wolf) **1:**29
chevrotain, water **2:**22
chickadee, black-capped **2:**23
chicken, greater prairie **2:**24
Chinese water deer **3:**15
chital (axis deer) **3:**14
chorus frog, northern **4:**12
chub **2:**25
chuckwalla **2:**26
cichlid, firemouth **2:**27
cichlid, lionhead **2:**28
civet, masked palm **2:**29
coati, ring-tailed **2:**30
cobra, king **2:**31
cockroach, wood **2:**32
cod, Atlantic **2:**33
coelacanth **2:**34
collared pika (Alaskan pika) **7:**23
colpeo fox **3:**43
column sponge, purple **9:**16
common backswimmer **1:**16
common bream **1:**42
common Cape girdled lizard **5:**34
common carp **2:**11
common dusky salamander **8:**13
common European prawn
    (palaemon) **7:**33
common European swallowtail
    9:29
common goose barnacle **1:**20
common goral **4:**34
common gray tree frog **4:**6
common gudgeon **4:**42

common langur **5**:30
common liver fluke **3**:39
common magpie moth **6**:35
common piddock **7**:21
common porpoise **7**:30
common roller **8**:9
common shelduck **8**:26
common shrew, Eurasian **8**:29
common toad, Eurasian **9**:42
common tree shrew **8**:28
conch, rooster-tail **2**:35
conger eel **3**:32
Congo catfish **2**:17
coolie loach **5**:43
coral, Devonshire cup **2**:36
coral, large star **2**:37
coral, northern stony **2**:38
coral, red precious **2**:39
coral, staghorn **2**:40
coral, star **2**:41
cordon-bleu (red-cheeked) waxbill **10**:30
corn bunting **2**:5
corn snake **8**:39
cottontail, New England **2**:42
courser, cream-colored **2**:43
crab-eating macaque **6**:9
cream-colored courser **2**:43
crested (warty) newt **6**:44
cricket, bush (bush katydid) **2**:44
cricket, European mole **3**:5
cricket, Mormon **3**:6
crimson-breasted barbet **1**:19
crossbill, red **3**:7
crosscut carpet shell **8**:27
crow, American **3**:8
crow, carrion **3**:9
crow, fish **3**:10
cup coral, Devonshire **2**:36

D

daboia (Russell's viper) **10**:20
dace **3**:11
daphnia (water flea) **3**:37
dark-green racer **7**:43
darner, blue-green **3**:12
darner, green **3**:13
deer, axis (chital) **3**:14
deer, Chinese water **3**:15
deer, fallow **3**:16
deer, pampas **3**:17
deer, red **3**:18
desert monitor **6**:27
Devonshire cup coral **2**:36
dhaman **3**:19
dog, African wild **3**:20
dogfish, spiny **3**:21
dollar, eccentric sand **3**:22
dolphin, Pacific white-sided **3**:23
dorcas gazelle **4**:23
Dory, European John **5**:25
double-banded sand grouse **4**:40
double-crested basilisk **1**:22
dove, laughing **3**:24
duck, torrent **3**:26
dung beetle, forest **1**:31
dunlin **3**:27
dusky salamander, common **8**:13
duster, magnificent feather **3**:28
duster, slime feather **3**:29
dwarf anteater **1**:13
dwarf mongoose **6**:24

E

eagle, tawny **3**:30
eastern malaria mosquito **6**:34
eccentric sand dollar **3**:22
echidna, long-nosed **3**:31
eel, conger **3**:32
Egyptian spiny mouse **6**:38
elephant, forest **3**:33
endangered animals
    anoa **1**:11
    cat, Iriomote **2**:14
    chamois **2**:21
    deer, pampas **3**:17
    dog, African wild **3**:20
    elephant, forest **3**:33
    gavial **4**:21
    gazelle, gazelle **4**:23

goat, wild **4**:32
guemal, Peruvian **4**:44
hog, pygmy **5**:15
horse, Przewalski's **5**:18
langur, common **5**:30
lemur, gentle gray **5**:32
moloch (silvery gibbon) **4**:28
monitor, desert **6**:27
monkey, Goeldi's **6**:30
monkey, woolly spider (muriqui) **6**:32
penguin, Galápagos **7**:16
pronghorn **7**:34
quetzal **7**:41
solenodon, Haitian **9**:8
stork, white **9**:25
turtle, giant South American river (arrau) **10**:14
epaulet bat, Gambian **1**:23
Eurasian beaver **1**:27
Eurasian bittern **1**:35
Eurasian common shrew **8**:29
Eurasian common toad **9**:42
Eurasian minnow **6**:21
Eurasian nuthatch **7**:5
Eurasian siskin **8**:30
European mink **6**:20
European mole **6**:20
European mole cricket **3**:5
European mouflon **6**:37
European perch **7**:18
European prawn, common (palaemon) **7**:33
European rhinoceros beetle **1**:30
European sole **9**:7
European spadefoot **9**:10
European swallowtail, common **9**:29
European tree frog **4**:7
European water vole **10**:23
European wild cat **2**:12
European wild rabbit **7**:42

F

fairy bluebird, blue-backed **1**:37
fallow deer **3**:16
false gavial **4**:22
feather duster, magnificent **3**:28
feather duster, slime **3**:29
featherworm, peacock **3**:34
filefish, orange-spotted **3**:35
finch, snow **3**:36
firemouth cichlid **2**:27
fire salamander **8**:14
fire sponge **9**:15
fish
    argus, blue-spotted **1**:15
    barb, half-banded **1**:18
    barracuda, Pacific **1**:21
    bitterling **1**:34
    bowfin **1**:41
    bream, common **1**:42
    butterflyfish, freshwater **2**:9
    carp, common **2**:11
    catfish, bronze **2**:16
    catfish, Congo **2**:17
    catfish, glass **2**:18
    catfish, shovelnose **2**:19
    cavefish, blind **2**:20
    chub **2**:25
    cichlid, firemouth **2**:27
    cichlid, lionhead **2**:28
    cod, Atlantic **2**:33
    coelacanth **2**:34
    dace **3**:11
    dogfish, spiny **3**:21
    eel, conger **3**:32
    filefish, orange-spotted **3**:35
    gourami, striped **4**:35
    gudgeon, common **4**:42
    John Dory, European **5**:25
    loach, coolie **5**:43
    loach, stone **5**:44
    lungfish, Australian **6**:8
    minnow, Eurasian **6**:21
    perch, European **7**:18
    piranha, white **7**:25
    reedfish **8**:6
    roach **8**:8
    ruby, black **8**:11

rudd **8**:12
shark, European angel **8**:22
shark, great hammerhead **8**:23
shark, Port Jackson **8**:24
sharksucker **8**:25
smelt, sand **8**:36
snipefish, longspine **9**:6
sole, European **9**:7
spadefish **9**:9
surgeonfish, powder-blue surgeon **9**:27
swordtail **9**:31
tetra, bleeding-heart **9**:38
tetra, glowlight **9**:39
triggerfish, redtooth **10**:11
triggerfish, undulate **10**:12
turbot **10**:13
unicornfish **10**:17
wels **10**:33
fish crow **3**:10
fishing (tentacled) snake **8**:44
flea, water (daphnia) **3**:37
flicker, red-shafted **3**:38
fluke, common liver **3**:39
fly, large bee **3**:40
flycatcher, fork-tailed **3**:41
flying possum, pygmy **7**:32
forest dung beetle **1**:31
forest elephant **3**:33
forest pig, giant **7**:22
fork-tailed flycatcher **3**:41
fox, African bat-eared **3**:42
fox, colpeo **3**:43
freshwater butterflyfish **2**:9
frog, agile **3**:44
frog, burrowing tree **4**:5
frog, common gray tree **4**:6
frog, European tree **4**:7
frog, gold **4**:8
frog, marbled reed **4**:9
frog, marsupial **4**:10
frog, moor **4**:11
frog, northern chorus **4**:12
frog, ornate horned **4**:13
frog, paradox **4**:14
frog, pickerel **4**:15
frog, pig **4**:16
frog, red-legged **4**:17
frog, strawberry poison dart **4**:18
fulmar, arctic **4**:19
fur seal, South American **8**:19

G

Gaboon viper **10**:19
Galápagos penguin **7**:16
Gambian epaulet bat **1**:23
gaur **4**:20
gavial **4**:21
gavial, false **4**:22
gazelle, dorcas **4**:23
gecko, blue-tailed day **4**:24
gecko, gliding **4**:25
gecko, Madagascar **4**:26
gecko, northern leaf-tailed **4**:27
gem anemone **1**:10
gentle gray lemur **5**:32
gentoo penguin **7**:17
Geoffroy's cat **2**:13
giant African scorpion **8**:16
giant African snail **8**:37
giant forest pig **7**:22
giant pangolin (scaly anteater) **1**:14
giant petrel, southern **7**:19
giant South American river turtle (arrau) **10**:14
giant tube sponge **9**:16
gibbon, silvery (moloch) **4**:28
gibbon, white-cheeked **4**:29
Gila monster **6**:33
giraffe, reticulated **4**:30
girdled lizard, common Cape **5**:34
glass catfish **2**:18
glass lizard, slender **5**:39
glider, yellow-bellied **4**:31
gliding gecko **4**:25
glowlight tetra **9**:39
goat, wild **4**:32
Goeldi's monkey **6**:30

golden-mantled ground squirrel **9**:20
goldenrod spider **9**:14
gold frog **4**:8
goose, magpie **4**:33
goose barnacle, common **1**:20
gopher snake **8**:40
gopher tortoise **10**:5
goral, common **4**:34
Gould's monitor **6**:28
gourami, striped **4**:35
grasshopper, blue-winged wasteland **4**:36
grasshopper, green valley **4**:37
grass snake **8**:41
gray lemur, gentle **5**:32
gray tree frog, common **4**:6
great black-backed gull **5**:5
greater bird of paradise **1**:33
greater kudu **5**:28
greater prairie chicken **2**:24
great gray owl **7**:8
great hammerhead shark **8**:22
green darner **3**:13
greenfinch **4**:38
greenshank **4**:39
green toad **9**:43
green tree python **7**:37
green valley grasshopper **4**:37
grenadier weaver (red bishop) **10**:32
grivet (savanna monkey) **6**:31
ground squirrel, golden-mantled **9**:20
grouse, double-banded sand **4**:40
guanaco **4**:41
gudgeon, common **4**:42
guemal, Peruvian **4**:44
guenon, moustached **4**:43
gull, great black-backed **5**:5

H

Haitian solenodon **9**:8
half-banded barb **1**:18
hammerhead shark, great **8**:23
hardun **5**:6
hare, arctic **5**:7
hartebeest **5**:8
hartebeest, hunter's (hirola) **5**:9
hawkmoth, broad-bordered bee **5**:10
hedgehog, Algerian **5**:11
hedgehog tenrec, lesser **9**:36
hedge sparrow **9**:12
helmeted lizard, smooth-headed **5**:40
helmeted turtle **10**:15
heron, little blue **5**:12
heron, purple **5**:14
Himalayan tahr **9**:32
hirola (hunter's hartebeest) **5**:9
Hoffmann's two-toed sloth **8**:33
hog, pygmy **5**:15
Honduran white bat **1**:24
hornbill, red-billed **5**:16
horned frog, ornate **4**:13
horntail, large **5**:17
horse, Przewalski's **5**:18
horsefly, cattle **5**:19
horsehair worm **10**:39
human-body louse **6**:7
hunter's hartebeest (hirola) **5**:9
hyrax, Cape **5**:20

I

ice cream cone worm **10**:40
imperial shag **8**:21
invertebrates, other
    anemone, opelet **1**:9
    anemone, silver-spotted (gem anemone) **1**:10
    barnacle, common goose **1**:20
    conch, rooster-tail **2**:35
    coral, Devonshire cup **2**:36
    coral, large star **2**:37
    coral, northern stony **2**:38
    coral, red precious **2**:39
    coral, staghorn **2**:40
    coral, star **2**:41
    dollar, eccentric sand **3**:22

duster, magnificent feather **3**:28
duster, slime feather **3**:29
featherworm, peacock **3**:34
fluke, common liver **3**:39
jellyfish, trumpet-stalked (stauromedusan) **5**:24
mussel, swan **6**:40
nettle, sea **6**:42
orange, sea **7**:7
paw, kitten's **7**:15
piddock, common **7**:21
razor, pod **7**:44
shell, crosscut carpet **8**:27
slug, red **8**:35
snail, giant African **8**:37
sponge, fire **9**:15
sponge, purple column (giant tube) **9**:16
sponge, stinker **9**:17
sponge, vase **9**:18
star, slime **9**:21
stentor, blue **9**:23
tapeworm, cat **9**:34
urchin, slate-pencil **10**:18
whelk, waved **10**:35
worm, horsehair **10**:39
worm, ice cream cone **10**:40
worm, peripatus velvet **10**:41
worm, red tube **10**:42
Iriomote cat **2**:14
Italian wall lizard **5**:35

J-K

jacamar, rufous-tailed **5**:21
jacana, wattled **5**:22
jackal, black-backed **5**:23
Japanese macaque **6**:10
Java sparrow **9**:13
jellyfish, trumpet-stalked (stauromedusan) **5**:24
John Dory, European **5**:25
katydid, bush (bush cricket) **2**:44
katydid, steppe **5**:26
keel-billed toucan **10**:8
king cobra **2**:31
king parrot **7**:14
kingsnake, prairie **5**:27
king vulture **10**:26
kitten's paw **7**:15
kudu, greater **5**:28
kudu, lesser **5**:29

L

langur, common **5**:30
lappet-faced vulture **10**:27
lapwing **5**:31
large, short-nosed bandicoot **1**:17
large bee fly **3**:40
large horntail **5**:17
large mouse-eared bat **1**:25
large star coral **2**:37
laughing dove **3**:24
leaf-cutter ant **1**:12
leaf-tailed gecko, northern **4**:27
legless lizard, California **5**:33
lemur, gentle gray **5**:32
lesser hedgehog tenrec **9**:36
lesser kudu **5**:29
lilac-breasted roller **8**:10
lionhead cichlid **2**:28
little blue heron **5**:12
little button quail **7**:40
liver fluke, common **3**:39
lizard, California legless **5**:33
lizard, common Cape girdled **5**:34
lizard, Italian wall **5**:35
lizard, lyre-headed **5**:36
lizard, sand **5**:37
lizard, short-horned **5**:38
lizard, slender glass **5**:39
lizard, smooth-headed helmeted **5**:40
lizard, southern alligator **5**:41
lizard, wall **5**:42
loach, coolie **5**:43
loach, stone **5**:44
locust, migratory **6**:5
long-nosed echidna **3**:31

longspine snipefish **9**:6
lorikeet, musk **6**:6
louse, human-body **6**:7
lungfish, Australian **6**:8
lyre-headed lizard **5**:36

M

macaque, crab-eating **6**:9
macaque, Japanese **6**:10
macaw, blue-and-yellow **6**:11
macaw, military **6**:12
Madagascar gecko **4**:26
magnificent feather duster **3**:28
magpie, azure-winged **6**:13
magpie goose **4**:33
magpie moth, common **6**:35
malaria mosquito, eastern **6**:34
mamba, black **6**:14
mammals
agouti, orange-rumped **1**:7
alpaca **1**:8
anoa **1**:11
anteater, dwarf **1**:13
anteater, scaly (giant pangolin) **1**:14
bandicoot, large, short-nosed **1**:17
bat, Gambian epaulet **1**:23
bat, Honduran white **1**:24
bat, large mouse-eared **1**:25
bear, sloth **1**:26
beaver, Eurasian **1**:27
blackbuck **1**:36
brocket, red **1**:43
buffalo, water **1**:44
bushbuck **2**:6
cat, European wild **2**:12
cat, Geoffroy's **2**:13
cat, Iriomote **2**:14
cat, ring-tailed **2**:15
chamois **2**:21
chevrotain, water **2**:22
civet, masked palm **2**:29
coati, ring-tailed **2**:15
cottontail, New England **2**:42
deer, axis (chital) **3**:14
deer, Chinese water **3**:15
deer, fallow **3**:16
deer, pampas **3**:17
deer, red **3**:18
dog, African wild **3**:20
dolphin, Pacific white-sided **3**:23
echidna, long-nosed **3**:31
elephant, forest **3**:33
fox, African bat-eared **3**:42
fox, colpeo **3**:43
gaur **4**:20
gazelle, dorcas **4**:23
gibbon, silvery (moloch) **4**:28
gibbon, white-cheeked **4**:29
giraffe, reticulated **4**:30
glider, yellow-bellied **4**:31
goat, wild **4**:32
goral, common **4**:34
guanaco **4**:41
guemal, Peruvian **4**:44
guenon, moustached **4**:43
hare, arctic **5**:7
hartebeest **5**:8
hedgehog, Algerian **5**:11
hirola (hunter's hartebeest) **5**:9
hog, pygmy **5**:15
horse, Przewalski's **5**:18
hyrax, Cape **5**:20
jackal, black-backed **5**:23
kudu, greater **5**:28
kudu, lesser **5**:29
langur, common **5**:30
lemur, gentle gray **5**:32
macaque, crab-eating **6**:9
macaque, Japanese **6**:10
marmot, Olympic **6**:16
mink, European **6**:20
mole, European **6**:22
mongoose, dwarf **6**:24
mongoose, white-tailed **6**:25
monkey, Goeldi's **6**:30
monkey, savanna (grivet) **6**:31

monkey, woolly spider (muriqui) **6**:32
mouflon, European **6**:37
mouse, Egyptian spiny **6**:38
mouse, wood **6**:39
narwhal **6**:41
olingo **7**:6
pademelon, red-legged **7**:12
pig, giant forest **7**:22
pika, collared (Alaskan pika) **7**:23
polecat, striped (zorilla) **7**:28
porcupine, tree **7**:29
porpoise, common **7**:30
possum, brush-tailed **7**:31
possum, pygmy flying **7**:32
pronghorn **7**:34
rabbit, European wild **7**:42
reedbuck, mountain **8**:5
reindeer (caribou) **8**:7
seal, Baikal **8**:18
seal, South American fur **8**:19
sea lion, Australian **8**:17
shrew, common tree **8**:28
shrew, Eurasian common **8**:29
sloth, Hoffmann's two-toed **8**:33
sloth, three-toed **8**:34
solenodon, Haitian **9**:8
springbok **9**:19
squirrel, golden-mantled ground **9**:20
suricate (meerkat) **9**:28
tahr, Himalayan **9**:32
tarsier, western **9**:35
tenrec, lesser hedgehog **9**:36
viscacha, plains **10**:22
vole, European water **10**:23
whale, Baird's beaked **10**:34
wolf, maned **10**:38
zebu **10**:44
manakin, red-capped **6**:15
maned wolf **10**:38
marbled reed frog **4**:9
marbled white **10**:36
marmot, Olympic **6**:16
marsupial frog **4**:10
martin, sand **6**:17
masked palm civet **2**:29
Mediterranean tortoise, spur-tailed **10**:6
meerkat (suricate) **9**:28
merganser, red-breasted **6**:19
migratory locust **6**:5
military macaw **6**:12
mink, European **6**:20
minnow, Eurasian **6**:21
mistle thrush **9**:40
mole, European **6**:22
mole cricket, European **3**:5
moloch (lizard) **6**:23
moloch (silvery gibbon) **4**:28
mongoose, dwarf **6**:24
mongoose, white-tailed **6**:25
monitor, Cape **6**:26
monitor, desert **6**:27
monitor, Gould's **6**:28
monitor, Nile **6**:29
monkey, Goeldi's **6**:30
monkey, savanna (grivet) **6**:31
monkey, woolly spider (muriqui) **6**:32
moor frog **4**:11
Mormon cricket **3**:6
mosquito, eastern malaria **6**:34
moth, common magpie **6**:35
moth, six-spot burnet **6**:36
mouflon, European **6**:37
mouse, Egyptian spiny **6**:38
mouse, wood **6**:39
mouse-eared bat, large **1**:25
moustached guenon **4**:43
muriqui (woolly spider monkey) **6**:32
musk lorikeet **6**:6
mussel, swan **6**:40

N

nankeen night heron **5**:13

monkey, woolly spider (muriqui) **6**:32
mouflon, European **6**:37
mouse, Egyptian spiny **6**:38
mouse, wood **6**:39
narwhal **6**:41
olingo **7**:6
pademelon, red-legged **7**:12
pig, giant forest **7**:22
pika, collared (Alaskan pika) **7**:23
polecat, striped (zorilla) **7**:28
porcupine, tree **7**:29
porpoise, common **7**:30
possum, brush-tailed **7**:31
possum, pygmy flying **7**:32
pronghorn **7**:34
rabbit, European wild **7**:42
reedbuck, mountain **8**:5
reindeer (caribou) **8**:7
seal, Baikal **8**:18
seal, South American fur **8**:19
sea lion, Australian **8**:17
shrew, common tree **8**:28
shrew, Eurasian common **8**:29
sloth, Hoffmann's two-toed **8**:33
sloth, three-toed **8**:34
solenodon, Haitian **9**:8
springbok **9**:19
squirrel, golden-mantled ground **9**:20
suricate (meerkat) **9**:28
tahr, Himalayan **9**:32
tarsier, western **9**:35
tenrec, lesser hedgehog **9**:36
viscacha, plains **10**:22
vole, European water **10**:23
whale, Baird's beaked **10**:34
wolf, maned **10**:38
zebu **10**:44

narwhal **6**:41
New England cottontail **2**:42
newt, alpine **6**:43
newt, crested (warty) **6**:44
night heron, nankeen **5**:13
Nile monitor **6**:29
northern chorus frog **4**:12
northern leaf-tailed gecko **4**:27
northern stony coral **2**:38
nuthatch, Eurasian **7**:5

O

oak treehopper **10**:10
olingo **7**:6
Olympic marmot **6**:16
opelet anemone **1**:9
orange-rumped agouti **1**:7
orange-spotted filefish **3**:35
oriental beauty snake **8**:42
oriental water dragon **3**:25
ornate horned frog **4**:13
owl, great gray **7**:8
owl, scops **7**:9
owl, short-eared **7**:10
owl, tawny **7**:11

P

Pacific barracuda **1**:21
Pacific white-sided dolphin **3**:23
pademelon, red-legged **7**:12
palaemon (common European prawn) **7**:33
palm civet, masked **2**:29
pampas deer **3**:17
pangolin, giant (scaly anteater) **1**:14
paradox frog **4**:14
parakeet, rose-ringed **7**:13
parrot, king **7**:14
peacock featherworm **3**:34
penguin, Galápagos **7**:16
penguin, gentoo **7**:17
perch, European **7**:18
peripatus velvet worm **10**:41
Peruvian guemal **4**:44
petrel, southern giant **7**:19
pheasant, Reeve's **7**:20
pickerel frog **4**:15
piddock, common **7**:21
pig, giant forest **7**:22
pig frog **4**:16
pika, collared (Alaskan pika) **7**:23
pin-tailed whydah **10**:37
pipe snake, red-tailed **8**:43
pipit, water **7**:24
piranha, white **7**:25
plains viscacha **10**:22
plover, spur-winged **7**:26
pochard, red-crested **7**:27
pod razor **7**:44
poison dart frog, strawberry **4**:18
polecat, striped (zorilla) **7**:28
porcupine, tree **7**:29
porpoise, common **7**:30
Port Jackson shark **8**:24
possum, brush-tailed **7**:31
possum, pygmy flying **7**:32
powder-blue surgeonfish **9**:27
prairie chicken, greater **2**:24
prairie kingsnake **5**:27
prawn, common European (palaemon) **7**:33
precious coral, red **2**:39
pronghorn **7**:34
Przewalski's horse **5**:18
puffin, tufted **7**:35
purple column sponge **9**:16
purple heron **5**:14
pygmy flying possum **7**:32
pygmy hog **5**:15
python, carpet **7**:36
python, green tree **7**:37
python, reticulate **7**:38
python, rock **7**:39

Q-R

quail, little button **7**:40
quetzal **7**:41

rabbit, European wild **7**:42
racer, dark-green **7**:43
razor, pod **7**:44
red-billed hornbill **5**:16
red bishop (grenadier weaver) **10**:32
red-breasted merganser **6**:19
red brocket **1**:43
red-capped manakin **6**:15
red-cheeked (cordon-bleu) waxbill **10**:30
red-crested pochard **7**:27
red crossbill **3**:7
red deer **3**:18
red-legged frog **4**:17
red-legged pademelon **7**:12
red precious coral **2**:39
red-shafted flicker **3**:38
red slug **8**:35
red-tailed pipe snake **8**:43
redtooth triggerfish **10**:11
red tube worm **10**:42
reedbuck, mountain **8**:5
reedfish **8**:6
reed frog, marbled **4**:9
Reeve's pheasant **7**:20
reindeer (caribou) **8**:7
reptiles
  adder **1**:5
  adder, rhombic night **1**:6
  basilisk, double-crested **1**:22
  chuckwalla **2**:26
  cobra, king **2**:31
  dhaman **3**:19
  dragon, oriental water **3**:25
  gavial **4**:21
  gavial, false **4**:22
  gecko, blue-tailed day **4**:24
  gecko, gliding **4**:25
  gecko, Madagascar **4**:26
  gecko, northern leaf-tailed **4**:27
  hardun **5**:6
  kingsnake, prairie **5**:27
  lizard, California legless **5**:33
  lizard, common Cape girdled **5**:34
  lizard, Italian wall **5**:35
  lizard, lizard **5**:37
  lizard, lyre-headed **5**:36
  lizard, short-horned **5**:38
  lizard, slender glass **5**:39
  lizard, smooth-headed helmeted **5**:40
  lizard, southern alligator **5**:41
  lizard, wall **5**:42
  mamba, black **6**:14
  moloch (lizard) **6**:23
  monitor, Cape **6**:26
  monitor, desert **6**:27
  monitor, Gould's **6**:28
  monitor, Nile **6**:29
  monster, Gila **6**:33
  python, carpet **7**:36
  python, green tree **7**:37
  python, reticulate **7**:38
  python, rock **7**:39
  racer, dark-green **7**:43
  skink, sand **8**:31
  skink, stump-tailed **8**:32
  snake, African twig **8**:38
  snake, corn **8**:39
  snake, gopher **8**:40
  snake, grass **8**:41
  snake, oriental beauty **8**:42
  snake, red-tailed pipe **8**:43
  snake, tentacled (fishing) **8**:44
  sungazer **9**:26
  tortoise, gopher **10**:5
  tortoise, spur-tailed Mediterranean **10**:6
  turtle, giant South American river (arrau) **10**:14
  turtle, helmeted **10**:15
  turtle, spotted **10**:16
  viper, Gaboon **10**:19
  viper, Russell's (daboia) **10**:20
reticulated giraffe **4**:30
reticulate python **7**:38
rhinoceros beetle, European **1**:30

rhombic night adder **1**:6
ring-tailed cat **2**:15
ring-tailed coati **2**:30
river turtle, giant South American (arrau) **10**:14
roach **8**:8
rock python **7**:39
rock thrush **9**:41
roller, common **8**:9
roller, lilac-breasted **8**:10
rooster-tail conch **2**:35
rose-ringed parakeet **7**:13
ruby, black **8**:11
rudd **8**:12
rufous-tailed jacamar **5**:21
Russell's viper (daboia) **10**:20

S

sail butterfly (scarce swallowtail) **2**:8
salamander, common dusky **8**:13
salamander, fire **8**:14
sand dollar, eccentric **3**:22
sand grouse, double-banded **4**:40
sand lizard **5**:37
sand martin **6**:17
sandpiper, wood **8**:15
sand skink **8**:31
sand smelt **8**:36
satin bower-bird **1**:40
savanna monkey (grivet) **6**:31
scaly anteater (giant pangolin) **1**:14
scarce swallowtail (sail butterfly) **2**:8
scarlet tanager **9**:33
scops owl **7**:9
scorpion, giant African **8**:16
seal, Baikal **8**:18
seal, South American fur **8**:19
sea lion, Australian **8**:17
sea nettle **6**:42
sea orange **7**:7
sexton (burying beetle) **8**:20
shag, imperial **8**:21
shark, European angel **8**:22
shark, great hammerhead **8**:23
shark, Port Jackson **8**:24
sharksucker **8**:25
shelduck, common **8**:26
shell, crosscut carpet **8**:27
short-eared owl **7**:10
short-horned lizard **5**:38
short-nosed bandicoot, large **1**:17
shovelnose catfish **2**:19
shrew, common tree **8**:28
shrew, Eurasian common **8**:29
silver-spotted anemone (gem anemone) **1**:10
silvery gibbon (moloch) **4**:28
sink, sand **8**:31
siskin, Eurasian **8**:30
six-spot burnet moth **6**:36
skink, stump-tailed **8**:32
slate-pencil urchin **10**:18
slender glass lizard **5**:39
slime feather duster **3**:29
slime star **9**:21
sloth, Hoffmann's two-toed **8**:33
sloth, three-toed **8**:34
sloth bear **1**:26
slug, red **8**:35
smelt, sand **8**:36
smooth-headed helmeted lizard **5**:40
snail, giant African **8**:37
snake, African twig **8**:38
snake, corn **8**:39
snake, fishing (tentacled) **8**:44
snake, gopher **8**:40
snake, grass **8**:41
snake, oriental beauty **8**:42
snake, red-tailed pipe **8**:43
snakefly **9**:5
snipefish, longspine **9**:6
snow finch **3**:36
sole, European **9**:7
solenodon, Haitian **9**:8
South American fur seal **8**:19

South American river turtle, giant (arrau) **10**:14
southern alligator lizard **5**:41
southern giant petrel **7**:19
spadefish **9**:9
spadefoot, European **9**:10
sparrow, hedge **9**:12
sparrow, Java **9**:13
spider, goldenrod **9**:14
spider monkey, woolly (muriqui) **6**:32
spiny dogfish **3**:21
spiny mouse, Egyptian **6**:38
sponge, fire **9**:15
sponge, purple column (giant tube) **9**:16
sponge, stinker **9**:17
sponge, vase **9**:18
spotted turtle **10**:16
springbok **9**:19
spur-tailed Mediterranean tortoise **10**:6
spur-winged plover **7**:26
squirrel, golden-mantled ground **9**:20
staghorn coral **2**:40
star, slime **9**:21
star coral **2**:41
star coral, large **2**:37
starling, superb **9**:22
stauromedusan (trumpet-stalked jellyfish) **5**:24
stentor, blue **9**:23
steppe katydid **5**:26
stinker sponge **9**:17
stonechat **9**:24
stone loach **5**:44
stony coral, northern **2**:38
stork, white **9**:25
strawberry poison dart frog **4**:18
striped gourami **4**:35
striped polecat (zorilla) **7**:28
stump-tailed skink **8**:32
sungazer **9**:26
superb blue wren **10**:43
superb starling **9**:22
surgeonfish, powder-blue **9**:27
suricate (meerkat) **9**:28
Surinam toad **9**:44
swallowtail, common European **9**:29
swallowtail, scarce (sail butterfly) **2**:8
swan, whooper **9**:30
swan mussel **6**:40
swordtail **9**:31

T

tahr, Himalayan **9**:32
tanager, scarlet **9**:33
tapeworm, cat **9**:34
tarsier, western **9**:35
tawny eagle **3**:30
tawny owl **7**:11
tenrec, lesser hedgehog **9**:36
tentacled (fishing) snake **8**:44
tern, whiskered **9**:37
tetra, bleeding-heart **9**:38
tetra, glowlight **9**:39
three-toed sloth **8**:34
thrush, mistle **9**:40
thrush, rock **9**:41
toad, Eurasian common **9**:42
toad, green **9**:43
toad, Surinam **9**:44
torrent duck **3**:26
tortoise, gopher **10**:5
tortoise, spur-tailed Mediterranean **10**:6
tortoiseshell **10**:7
toucan, keel-billed **10**:8
tree frog, burrowing **4**:5
tree frog, common gray **4**:6
tree frog, European **4**:7
treehopper **10**:9
treehopper, oak **10**:10
tree porcupine **7**:29
tree shrew, common **8**:28
tree sparrow, American tree **9**:11

triggerfish, redtooth **10**:11
triggerfish, undulate **10**:12
trumpet-stalked jellyfish (stauromedusan) **5**:24
tube sponge, giant **9**:16
tube worm, red **10**:42
tufted puffin **7**:35
turbot **10**:13
turtle, giant South American river (arrau) **10**:14
turtle, helmeted **10**:15
turtle, spotted **10**:16
twig snake, African **8**:38
two-toed sloth, Hoffmann's **8**:33

U-V

undulate triggerfish **10**:12
unicornfish **10**:17
urchin, slate-pencil **10**:18
vase sponge **9**:18
velvet worm, peripatus **10**:41
viper, Gaboon **10**:19
viper, Russell's (daboia) **10**:20
vireo, white-eyed **10**:21
viscacha, plains **10**:22
vole, European water **10**:23
vulture, American black **10**:24
vulture, bearded **10**:25
vulture, king **10**:26
vulture, lappet-faced **10**:27

W

wagtail, white **10**:28
wagtail, yellow **10**:29
wall lizard **5**:42
wall lizard, Italian **5**:35
warty (crested) newt **6**:44
wasteland grasshopper, blue-winged **4**:36
water buffalo **1**:44
water chevrotain **2**:22
water dragon, oriental **3**:25
water flea (daphnia) **3**:37
water measurer **6**:18
water pipit **7**:24
water vole, European **10**:23
wattled jacana **5**:22
waved whelk **10**:35
waxbill, red-cheeked (cordon-bleu) **10**:30
waxwing, cedar **10**:31
weaver, grenadier (red bishop) **10**:32
wels **10**:33
western tarsier **9**:35
whale, Baird's beaked **10**:34
whelk, waved **10**:35
whirligig beetle **1**:32
whiskered tern **9**:37
white, marbled **10**:36
white bat, Honduran **1**:24
white-cheeked gibbon **4**:29
white-eyed vireo **10**:21
white piranha **7**:25
white-sided dolphin, Pacific **3**:23
white stork **9**:25
white-tailed mongoose **6**:25
white wagtail **10**:28
whooper swan **9**:30
whydah, pin-tailed **10**:37
wild cat, European **2**:12
wild dog, African **3**:20
wild goat **4**:32
wolf, maned **10**:38
wood cockroach **2**:32
wood mouse **6**:39
wood sandpiper **8**:15
woolly spider monkey (muriqui) **6**:32
worm, horsehair **10**:39
worm, ice cream cone **10**:40
worm, peripatus velvet **10**:41
worm, red tube **10**:42

X-Y-Z

yellow-bellied glider **4**:31
yellow wagtail **10**:29
zebu **10**:44
zorilla (striped polecat) **7**:28